state of world population 2008

Reaching Common Ground: Culture, Gender and Human Rights

WITHDRAWN

United Nations Population Fund
Thoraya Ahmed Obaid, Executive Director

state of world population 2008
Reaching Common Ground:
Culture, Gender and Human Rights

On the cover
Dancers on a street in Salvador, Brazil.

© Peter Adams/Getty Images

Reaching Common Ground: Culture, Gender and Human Rights

Background image:
Cuban woman holding baby in her arms.

© J. Royan/Still Pictures

Nepalese family.
© Peter Bruyneel

Overview

Culture is and always has been central to development. As a natural and fundamental dimension of people's lives, culture must be integrated into development policy and programming. This report shows how this process works in practice.

The starting point of the report is the universal validity of the international human rights framework. The focus is therefore on discussing and showcasing how culturally sensitive approaches are critical for the realization of human rights in general and women's rights in particular.

The report gives an overview of the conceptual frameworks as well as the practice of development, looking at the everyday events that make up people's experience of development. Culturally sensitive approaches call for cultural fluency – familiarity with how cultures work, and how to work with them. The report presents some of the challenges and dilemmas of culturally sensitive strategies and suggests how partnerships can address them.

Culture – inherited patterns of shared meanings and common understandings – influences how people manage their lives, and provides the lens through which they interpret their society. Cultures affect how people think and act; but they do not produce uniformity of thought or behaviour.

Cultures must be seen in their wider context: They influence and are influenced by external circumstances and change in response. They are not static; people are continuously involved in reshaping them, although some aspects of culture continue to influence choices and lifestyles for very long periods.

Cultural customs, norms, behaviours and attitudes are as varied as they are elusive and dynamic. It is risky to generalize, and it is particularly dangerous to judge one culture by the norms and values of another. Such over-simplification can lead to the assumption that every member of a culture thinks the same way. This is not only a mistaken perception but ignores one of the drivers of cultural change, which is multiple expressions of internal resistance, out of which transitions emerge. The movement towards gender equality is a good example of this process at work.

Appeals for cultural sensitivity and engagement are sometimes wrongly interpreted as acceptance of harmful traditional practices, or a way of making excuses for non-compliance with universal human rights. This is far from the case – such relativism provides no basis for action and produces only stalemate and frustration. Values and practices that infringe upon human rights can be found in all cultures. Culturally sensitive approaches determine what makes sense to people and work with that knowledge. Embracing cultural realities can reveal the most effective ways to challenge harmful cultural practices and strengthen positive ones.

Culturally sensitive approaches:

• go beyond "what" to "how" and "why" things are the way they are;

• seek the local knowledge and relationships that can provide the basis for dialogue and positive change;

• avoid generalizations and acknowledge differences in values and objectives, even within the same culture;

• encourage humility among those who work with communities; and

• ensure that deep understanding of human realities, including culture, rather than theories or assumptions, become the basis for policy.

Culturally sensitive approaches are both logical and practical, recognizing that cultural development is as much a right as economic or social development. Creative solutions abound within cultures, and culturally sensitive approaches seek them out and work with them. Culturally sensitive approaches are crucial for understanding local contexts – involving legal, political, economic and social power relations – and their implications for development.

Human Rights

In addition to the Universal Declaration of Human Rights (1948), Member States of the United Nations have adopted a wide range of instruments elaborating on the principles of universality, indivisibility, interdependence, equality and non-discrimination. Once they enter into force, countries agree to be bound by their provisions; the fundamental provisions are binding on all nations. These instruments

are joined by consensus documents such as the International Conference on Population and Development Programme of Action (1994) and the Platform for Action of the Fourth World Conference on Women (1995).

There has been considerable discussion over the universality of human rights, but the discussion has often overlooked the critical interrelationships between human rights and cultures. The human rights framework includes protections for the collective rights of groups as well as those of individuals; among these is the right to health, including reproductive health. The language of rights is the language of resistance to deprivation and oppression, which is common to all cultures: People have begun using the language of rights to make their own claims.

Universal rights are realized by specific people and groups in their own cultural contexts, and must be understood in that way. This realization is what culturally sensitive approaches aim to achieve.

Culturally sensitive approaches recognize that:

• people in different cultures understand rights in different ways;

• people in the same culture also have different perspectives on and experiences of rights;

• people advocate for rights in ways that suit their cultural contexts;

• human rights can be ingrained through "cultural legitimacy"; and

• facilitating cultural legitimacy requires cultural knowledge and engagement.

Culturally sensitive approaches can provide tools for understanding how human rights and cultures interact. People will respect human rights which they see as culturally legitimate, but ensuring legitimacy calls for important safeguards:

• Avoid imposing particular interpretations of rights which undermine cultural ownership.

• Do not avoid struggles over the meanings of rights but acknowledge them.

• Contribute to policies by taking local norms and practices seriously into account.

- Understand cultures at local, national and international levels, and the interrelationships among them.

Culturally sensitive approaches call for the inclusion of all societies and reaching into communities, including marginalized groups within communities. This is not a swift or predictable process. Human development with full realization of human rights depends on serious and respectful engagement with cultures.

Women's Empowerment and Gender Equality

At a variety of international meetings and conferences since 1975, governments, civil society and United Nations bodies have committed themselves to work with and for women, with specific goals and targets, most recently the Millennium Development Goals in 2000. Yet gender inequality remains widespread and deep-rooted in many cultures. Women and girls are three fifths of the world's one billion poorest people, women are two thirds of the 960 million adults in the world who cannot read, and girls are 70 per cent of the 130 million children who are out of school. Some social and cultural norms and traditions perpetuate gender-based violence, and women and men can both learn to turn a blind eye or accept it. Indeed, women may defend the structures that oppress them.

Power operates within cultures through coercion that may be visible, hidden in the structures of government and the law or ingrained in the perceptions people have of themselves. Power relations are therefore the glue which holds and moulds gender dynamics, and underpins both the rationale and the way cultures interact and manifest themselves. Practices such as child marriage (which is a leading cause of obstetric fistula and maternal death) and female genital mutilation or cutting (which has severe health consequences) continue in many countries despite laws against them. Women may join in perpetuating these practices, believing them to be a form of protection for their children and themselves.

Advances in gender equality have never come without cultural struggle. Women in Latin America, for example, have succeeded in making gender violence visible and in securing legislation against it, but enforcement remains a problem.

UNFPA's approach to programming for women's empowerment and gender equality integrates human rights, gender mainstreaming and cultural sensitivity, encouraging transformative cultural change from within. UNFPA collaborates not only with governments but with a variety of local organizations and individuals, many of whom it identifies as agents of change.

The "culture lens" is UNFPA's tool for contesting gender inequality and building alliances. It helps to develop the cultural fluency needed for negotiating, persuading and cultivating cultural acceptance and ownership.

Culturally sensitive approaches must respond to variations in needs, experiences and cultures; must understand how people negotiate their own contexts; and must learn from local resistance. Approaches must be reflective, critical and comprehensive.

Reproductive Health and Reproductive Rights

People and communities give a wide variety of meanings to reproductive health and reproductive rights, and understandings may vary even among individuals within a community. Cultural sensitivity is about realizing and understanding these varied meanings and being prepared for some unexpected realities; for example, some men may work for gender equality against their apparent self-interest, and some women may support practices that apparently harm them. Culturally sensitive approaches seek to understand and work with a community's views about what men and women contribute to procreation; for example, what it signifies when a woman or a couple does not reproduce, the effect of contraception on a woman's ability to conceive or on a man's view of what makes up his "manhood". Such understanding is essential for effective cooperation.

Cultural sensitivity helps to mitigate and overcome resistance to couples and individuals voluntarily planning the timing, spacing and size of their families. It prepares the way for empowering women, in particular with control over their own fertility. Culturally sensitive approaches are essential tools for development organizations concerned with promoting sexual and reproductive health.

Culturally sensitive approaches are also critical in mobilizing communities and building partnerships to work against certain harmful traditional practices, notably female genital mutilation or cutting (FGM/C). Most national governments, local communities and the international community at large firmly stand against FGM/C as a violation of human rights and a danger to physical and mental health. It is, however, a widespread and deeply-rooted tradition among some communities, sometimes backed by a totally spurious interpretation of religious teaching. It may be considered essential for full entry into adulthood and membership in the community; women without it may be considered ugly and unclean. Ending the practice involves taking all the different cultural meanings into account and finding meaningful alternatives, in close cooperation and discussion with the community.

> *[W]e are reviewing our experience to enable us to respond to the cultural challenge: to help countries, communities and individuals interpret universal principles, translate them into culturally sensitive terms and design programmes based on them, programmes that people can really feel are their own.*

> *We can succeed in this if we keep close to our hearts the conviction that each human life is uniquely valuable, and that the right to development is the right for men and women to express the full measure of their humanity.*

> —Thoraya Ahmed Obaid, Executive Director, UNFPA

In recognizing and supporting local efforts, it is important to make alliances with opinion-makers and leaders as well as with those whose work in the field gives them significant outreach and influence. Some of the most dramatic changes occur when the guardians of cultural norms and practices, the "gatekeepers", are advocates for women's rights. In Cambodia, Buddhist nuns and monks are prominent in the struggle to combat HIV; in Zimbabwe, local leaders have taken up the challenge. Successful alliances seek broad partnerships in areas of human rights and gender equality, and set standards to apply in specific areas such as HIV prevention and AIDS treatment and care. Cultural sensitivity also necessitates taking into account the many other local efforts for change by organizations such as women's, youth and workers' groups and the ways they work with and reinforce each other.

Religion is central to many people's lives, and an important dimension of culture which influences the most intimate decisions and actions. Appeals to religion can be used to justify cultural practices such as killings in the name of "honour" or "crimes of passion", which are blatant human rights violations. Cultural sensitivity entails support for the many women – and some men – within the society who contest the practice.

Culturally sensitive approaches are essential for reaching the Millennium Development Goals, which includes a target, under Goal 5, to reduce the maternal mortality ratio by 75 per cent. The numbers of women dying as a consequence of pregnancy and childbirth are essentially unchanged since the 1980s, at about 536,000. Many times that number, between 10 and 15 million, suffer injury or illness. Lower maternal mortality, and avoiding injuries such as obstetric fistula, depends on better care in pregnancy and childbirth, emergency services in cases of complications and access to family planning. Cultural sensitivity is essential for success in these critical initiatives.

Engaging men in the design, implementation and delivery of programmes, for instance, is a means as well as the result of culturally sensitive approaches, and is a requirement of any development process intended to change behaviours and attitudes. Gender inequality and negative male attitudes are generally seen as a challenge to reproductive health and rights. Closer attention to men's experiences of gender and its inequalities is one of the building blocks of culturally sensitive approaches.

Cultural constructions of masculinity and sexuality can increase risk-taking and reduce the likelihood of men seeking help. Men tend to engage in sex at a younger age and have more partners than women; this may be connected with society's expectations of what makes a "real" man, and encourages risky sexual behaviour. Some men may be less concerned about their health than their masculinity. Cultural constructions increase stress and pressure on some men to prove themselves by exerting "male" authority, to the extent of forcing themselves on unwilling women. Their behaviour damages not only women's health but their social personalities – raped women have been forced to marry their rapists, or even accused of adultery.

Men may view seeking help or even information as a sign of weakness. They are much less likely than women

▲ *Universal access to education and health care helps all.*
© UNICEF/HQ06-1355/Claudio Versiani

to submit to voluntary counselling and testing for HIV. Male ignorance and anxiety puts both women and men at risk, but men may not see their behaviour as risky. Social and economic factors are also important: In communities where poverty, drugs and guns are common, HIV and AIDS take their place alongside other risks.

Culturally sensitive approaches go beyond standard explanations of male behaviour to investigate the relationship among social, political and legal contexts and resulting cultural norms, and the conditions under which men and women resist them. Building on this knowledge with local initiatives enables targeted and measured development support.

Poverty, Inequality and Population

The International Conference on Population and Development (ICPD) Programme of Action is the basis for achieving population objectives, on which development depends. ICPD goals, now incorporated in the Millennium Development Goals (MDGs), include universal access to reproductive health care, universal education, the empowerment of women and gender equality. Marginalized communities benefit least from development policies, and are more likely to be poor. Their education and health care are not as good and their lives are shorter than those of the better-off. Poorer women in particular are bound by harmful aspects of tradition and culture, with higher risks of maternal death, illness and injury.

Unequal "development" increases the extent and the depth of poverty. Low levels of health and education make it more difficult to translate any additional income into improved well-being, preventing people from setting or reaching personal goals. Gender relations and physical capacities also have an impact in determining access to opportunities and resources and the ability to enjoy human rights. Analysing people's choices in their local conditions and contexts is therefore a precondition for better policies.

Population issues come down to decisions people make in specific cultural contexts, for example, about family planning, education, health care and migration. Compared with the rural past, development has redefined the value of children. Smaller families and more investment per child have become the norm, and cultures have adapted accordingly, aided by better reproductive health and other services. Poor people may still want larger families, because their circumstances have changed less. Many have yet to see how smaller families and better health and education can benefit them.

Some poorer women do want fewer children, but cultural constraints hold them back. Taking that into account, family planning programmes can succeed even where there has been little economic development, as in Bangladesh. On the other hand, some poor women use contraception because they cannot afford children, rather than to protect their own reproductive health.

The key to reproductive health is making motherhood safer via (1) access to family planning to reduce unintended pregnancies and to space intended pregnancies; (2) skilled care for all pregnancies and births; (3) timely obstetric care for complications during childbirth; and (4) skilled care for women and babies after delivery.

The more likely it is that a woman will give birth with a skilled attendant present, the better the outcome is likely to be. Poorer women and poorer countries with lower proportions of attended births have higher rates of maternal mortality and morbidity. A woman may choose a traditional rather than a skilled birth attendant because the former provides a range of services before and after delivery, and because she is more familiar with the woman and her culture. Providing skilled birth attendants who have a cultural connection with the women they serve, as well as effective emergency and obstetric care backup and referral, which are also culturally acceptable, is a challenge for reproductive health services.

Migration has been a mixed experience for all concerned. International migrants – some 191 million in 2005 – provide at least $251 billion annually in remittances home, with appreciable effects on household and national economies. Their contribution is cultural as well as economic; migrants pick up and transmit cultural messages in both host and sending communities, including attitudes to human rights and gender equality.

Host countries' migration policies often have to contend with misunderstanding, discrimination and hostility towards migrants; source countries deal with the loss of skilled, qualified workers as well as family and community members. Trafficking, the dark underside of migration, damages both communities and the individuals concerned. It is becoming more common as migration policies become more restrictive, exposing migrants to economic exploitation, physical abuse and violence. These conditions provide fertile ground for conflicting cultural discourses. These include the reinvention of tradition (some of which entail perpetuating harmful practices such as FGM/C) among some groups of migrants, who feel alienated by the physical distance from their cultures of origin, while also marginalized by their host cultures.

Internal migration produces a range of risks and opportunities, weighted towards risk for the poor in both native and migrant populations. Better urban services, including reproductive health, are offset by their cost and the migrants' lack of social networks. Many migrants go home to give birth, despite apparently poorer-quality care.

The cumulative impact of economic and social change is forcing cultures to change in response. But the process may not be swift, and successful adaptation depends on understanding what is happening. Cultural change can itself change the social, political and economic context that produced it, and traditions and systems of meaning can survive many changes.

War, Gender Equality and Women's Empowerment

Women become a target in war because of their perceived position as guardians of culture. Rape is an act of violence aimed not only at a woman but at the cultural composition of her national or community identity. Communities may view raped women as tainted or worthless, and they may suffer further violence as a result. Few communities address gender-based violence openly, and women often do not talk about it.

Militarization of a culture works against women's empowerment and gender equality, partly through the increased incidence – and acceptability – of violence. Conflict imposes additional responsibilities and costs on women who may become heads of household in the absence of men. Men may feel themselves powerless and unable to fulfil their duty to protect their families. This can arouse male resentment and violence.

Women's human rights are an international security concern, accepted as such by the United Nation's Security Council resolution 1325 (2000), which also recognizes the need for cultural engagement to ensure that women are part of the peace process. Despite concerns about what is missing from UNSC 1325, it recognizes critical policy gaps and calls for change.

Cultural sensitivity is required by those engaged in development and humanitarian assistance when working with women who have coped with the stresses brought on by armed conflict. Culturally sensitive approaches target both the potential and actual deterioration in gender relations, and aim to protect whatever progress women have made towards gender equality, including women's reproductive health and rights. Culturally sensitive approaches are especially needed in the context of armed conflict, which challenges cultural expectations of masculinity such as men's responsibility for protecting their families.

Male frustration and impotence in the face of wartime hardships often turn against women, but the common perception of women as victims and men as aggressors does not describe the varied responsibilities that women take on in wartime as heads of household, breadwinners, caregivers and combatants. Policies and approaches must recognize this complexity. Failure to recognize people's resilience and resourcefulness and what has changed as a result of the conflict may exclude women and minorities, including people with disabilities, from involvement in setting post-conflict priorities and development strategies.

Culturally sensitive approaches are also needed for people coping with trauma, meeting refugees' needs for sexual and reproductive health care, building partnerships with local organizations and helping people retain or recover their sense of cultural identity amid the ravages of war.

Inclusive strategic partnerships are a cornerstone of culturally sensitive approaches. These are built on recognizing that creative interventions on and around human rights often necessitate meaningful participation from communities built on an appreciation of symbols, forms and powerful agents of communication.

Conclusions

- *International development agencies ignore culture – or marginalize it – at their peril. Advancing human rights requires an appreciation of the complexity, fluidity and centrality of culture by intentionally identifying and partnering with local agents of change.*

- *Approaches based on cultural knowledge provide viability to policymaking – and enable the "cultural politics" required for human rights.*

- *Cultural fluency determines how systems of meanings, economic and political opposition, or supportive policies develop – and can be developed.*

- *To develop cultural fluency, UNFPA proposes a "culture lens" as a programming tool.*

- *Culturally sensitive approaches investigate how variables such as economic status, politics, law, class, age, gender, religion and ethnicity intersect and lead to divergent understandings and manifestations of power.*

- *Culturally sensitive approaches call for different analytical and operational frameworks, and for introspection within the development community.*

1 Negotiating Culture: An Introduction

The implementation of the recommendations contained in the Programme of Action of the International Conference on Population and Development is the sovereign right of each country, consistent with national laws and development priorities, with full respect for the various religious and ethical values and cultural backgrounds of its people, and in conformity with universally recognized international human rights.

—International Conference on Population and Development Programme of Action, Principles[1]

Why Culture?

Earlier *State of World Population* reports have covered policy themes such as gender equality, women's empowerment, reproductive health, migration, urbanization and poverty.[2] This report incorporates these themes and draws attention to ways that development can work on behalf of cultural groups and minorities, with women's empowerment and gender equality especially in mind. This is a critical but neglected area.

Cultures help to mould the ways people live with each other and influence their understandings of and approaches to development. UNFPA's (United Nations Population Fund) experience shows that culturally sensitive programming is essential for achieving the goals of the 1994 International Conference on Population and Development (ICPD) Programme of Action, and of the Millennium Development Goals (MDGs) – that is, for development in conformity with human rights. Culturally sensitive approaches are tools to build ownership of human rights within communities.

The report's starting point is the universal validity and application of the international human rights framework. Cultural values should harmonize with human rights expectations; in fact, human rights may be described as universal cultural values – values that all cultures hold in common. Individual human rights enhance rather than conflict with the interests of the wider society – the human rights of the

◀ *A young woman in early labour and her partner wait outside the maternity clinic on the outskirts of Portoviejo, Ecuador. One of the functions of culture is to nurture and protect present and future generations.*
© Carina Wint

group as a whole. Some practices sanctioned by tradition are in conflict with human rights. Resolution of these tensions strengthens cultures and enriches individual lives.

This implies that human rights are not to be interpreted through a particular cultural lens: They are to be interpreted by all cultures.

Cultures change – they adapt to changing circumstances. While the impetus for change may come from external circumstances, change comes from within, through dynamics specific to the culture. Cooperation with development agencies like UNFPA can help to smooth the process of cultural adaptation in conformity with human rights. Assistance is especially valuable in a rapidly changing set of external circumstances such as climate change or economic globalization.

Change should not disturb cultural integrity. At times cultures need to defend themselves from the impact of external circumstances. External cooperation can assist in this case, too.

Human beings are social, but approaches to development often emphasize the ways in which people function as individuals rather than in their social context. Human development depends on individual access to assets and opportunities; but, it also depends on the quality of social relationships, which are embedded in cultures.[3]

Gender equality is a human right.[4] In all cultures there are pressures towards and against women's empowerment and gender equality. This report's most important conclusion is that culturally sensitive approaches are critical for realizing human rights and development.

Background

The State of World Population 2008 shares the principles of earlier United Nations Educational, Scientific and Cultural Organization (UNESCO) and United Nations Development Programme (UNDP) reports (see box 1). It is important to analyse and understand the varied roles of culture in social relationships and the ways in which culture influences individual and social choices. This report, however, focuses on putting culturally sensitive approaches into practice. The report addresses some of the everyday circumstances in which culture affects not only social relationships, but development issues such as gender inequalities, maternal health, fertility, ageing and poverty.

---

1 **UNESCO AND UNDP ON CULTURE**

In 1995, UNESCO's report, *Our Creative Diversity,*[5] suggested that a linear economic approach had obstructed creative cultural solutions and resulted in cultural tensions and frustrations. Human development required the enhancement of capabilities and the enrichment of lives through cultural expression and practice: "Culture is a constitutive part of human development." The report called for new global ethics; a commitment to pluralism and to facilitating artistic creativity; cultural accountability in media representations; attention to women's rights, including their reproductive freedom and political participation; addressing the rights of children and young people; pre-

serving cultural heritage; and culturally rooted solutions for protecting the environment. The report sought to expand the notion of cultural policymaking beyond the arts and cultural industries to ensuring that individuals and communities have the freedom to build their capabilities and express and practice their cultures.

UNDP's 2004 *Human Development Report: Cultural Liberty in Today's Diverse World*[6] also celebrated cultural diversity and stressed the importance of cultural inclusion. It reiterated that human development requires human rights and the deepening of democracy, as well as multicultural policies that allow people

to be who they are and want to be. The report countered notions that cultural plurality inevitably leads to conflict and that cultural rights are inherently superior to political and economic rights. It provided recommendations for how states could work to accommodate cultural diversities, such as by learning from new models of multicultural democracy — which have been useful for addressing deep-rooted injustices — and implementing power-sharing arrangements in order to resolve tensions.

Source: UNFPA. 2008. *Integrating Culture, Gender and Human Rights in Programming: A Training Manual.* New York: UNFPA.

In Indonesia, for example, UNFPA has been working with the Ministry of Women's Empowerment and selected civil society partners to reduce violence against women. During the anti-Soeharto demonstrations in 1988, sexual assaults – including rape, particularly against minority women – were widely reported; but violence against women was not new, and it continued when the disturbances died down. It was rooted in cultural norms and practices that placed a low value on women. Many women had come to accept their position: "The concept of gender-based violence, particularly domestic violence, often does not resonate within Indonesian society, and is not readily identified, even among many victims themselves. Women who do recognize themselves as survivors of violence often remain silent because of the dishonour associated with this taboo."[7]

Cultural awareness and engagement were critical to effecting change. UNPFA built partnerships with rights-oriented religious institutions and others already working for change, reaching people in their own language through familiar, respected cultural media.

Puan Amal Hayati, a group of feminist Muslims and intellectuals formed in response to the crisis, uses Islamic teachings and values to empower women, prevent violence against them and provide services for survivors. Members work with Islamic boarding schools, *pesantrens,* which ensures a wide audience. The leaders of the *pesantrens,* both male and female, are very popular in the communities and are well-placed to set good examples of more equitable male-female relationships.[8]

This approach goes to the root of cultural perceptions that legitimize male power over women and bring some women to accept the power relations that harm them. The approach is characterized by cultural fluency, which means familiarity with a culture: its nature and how it works in times of conflict and harmony. Cultural fluency means awareness of several dimensions of culture, including communication; ways of naming, framing and taming conflict; approaches to meaning formation; and identities and roles.[9]

2 UNFPA: *TIPS TO CULTURALLY SENSITIVE PROGRAMMING*

- *Invest time in knowing the culture in which you are operating.*
- *Hear what the community has to say.*
- *Demonstrate respect.*
- *Show patience.*
- *Gain the support of local power structures.*
- *Be inclusive.*
- *Provide solid evidence.*
- *Rely on the objectivity of science.*
- *Avoid value judgements.*
- *Use language sensitively.*
- *Work through local allies.*
- *Assume the role of facilitator.*
- *Honour commitments.*
- *Know your adversaries.*
- *Find common ground.*
- *Accentuate the positive.*
- *Use advocacy to effect change.*
- *Create opportunities for women.*
- *Build community capacity.*
- *Reach out through popular culture.*
- *Let people do what they do best.*
- *Nurture partnerships.*
- *Celebrate achievements.*
- *Never give up.*

Source: UNFPA. 2004. *Guide to Working from Within: 24 Tips for Culturally Sensitive Programming.* New York: UNFPA. http://www.unfpa.org/culture/24tips/cover.htm>.

Culture is a matrix of infinite possibilities and choices. From within the same culture matrix we can extract arguments and strategies for the degradation and ennoblement of our species, for its enslavement or liberation, for the suppression of its productive potential or its enhancement.[10]

This report shows that culturally sensitive approaches must be integrated with economic, political, social and other explanations to develop a comprehensive picture of how people function within their social contexts and why they make the choices they do. As the example from Indonesia shows, cultural knowledge comes from patient and committed engagement, developing partnerships and policies that work with change from within. In every culture, there are people who contest harmful practices and develop home-grown solutions, and who may be helped and strengthened by dialogue and new ideas. Supporting those who share development priorities and goals, particularly a commitment to human rights, is often the most effective way of securing meaningful and lasting changes in social relationships.

The report emphasizes that culturally sensitive approaches have a critical role in "progress towards achieving international development goals and advancing human rights".[11] It recommends careful analysis and provides examples of culturally sensitive approaches. It presents some of the practical challenges and dilemmas of culturally sensitive strategies and uses case reports to show how development agencies have been working in partnerships to address them.

What Is Culture?

Culture is made up of inherited patterns of meanings that people share within particular contexts.[12] Through socialization, people develop common understandings of what is significant and what is not. These common understandings, which may be reflected in symbols, values, norms, beliefs, relationships and different forms of creative expression,[13] influence how people "manage their daily worlds, large and small";[14] they "shape the way things are done and understandings of why they should be done so";[15] they provide the lens through which people interpret their society.[16]

However, this does not mean that people who share the same cultures manage their daily worlds in identical ways; for, although cultures "affect how people line up and how they act on a wide range of matters",[17] they do not produce uniformity of thought or behaviour.

> *UNESCO's Universal Declaration on Cultural Diversity (2001), approved by 190 member states, defines culture as "The set of distinctive spiritual, material, intellectual and emotional features of society or a social group. [It] encompasses, in addition to art and literature, lifestyles, ways of living together, value systems, traditions and beliefs."*[20]

▲ *A woman and her children in their village near Quito, Ecuador.*
© Ed Darack/Getty Images

"Individuals who live within the same cultural setting can hold antagonistic convictions, based on different values."[18] However, these varied values and interactions are part of a cultural system that provides the "language that makes understanding [the ways of life within it] possible".[19]

Interpretations of culture should be qualified in two important respects.

- *First, it is important to locate cultures in their contexts.* Cultures are linked to the availability of resources; levels and types of technology and knowledge; modes of production and the structures and relationships of power that are generated to manage them; inherited philosophies and religion; people's perceptions of their and others' place and space in society and the world; and mechanisms and types of socialization. Cultures are part of a wider picture; they influence and are influenced by their contexts and change within the overall context. This "dynamic and interactive"[21] dimension is important for understanding the roles of culture in development.

• *Second, cultures are not static.* People are continuously involved in reshaping cultures through their interactions. It is important, however, not to overestimate the speed with which cultures change. Some aspects of culture continue to influence choices and lifestyles for very long periods;[22] people may maintain their attachment to shared ways of living, particularly when they believe that their cultural identities and particular frames of reference are being threatened. Learned norms, behaviours, beliefs and values – particularly those absorbed in childhood – can have long-term influence, though their significance will vary. Broader factors can inhibit cultural fluidity and restrict the growth of shared understandings, expectations and norms, for example, where people have limited opportunities to socialize beyond their immediate contexts; where they lack access to information or the ability to take advantage of it; or where they are denied the economic, social, political and cultural rights that would allow them to expand their range of choices.

What Culture Is Not...

The different definitions and uses made of culture have presented serious problems for analysis, communication and action. For example, culture is often defined in terms of customs, norms, styles of dress, tastes in food and forms of artistic expression. These manifestations of culture are important, but an exclusive focus on them makes it easy to miss the substance.

Distinctions based on value judgments are risky, for example, "traditional" and "modern"; the "first" and the "third" worlds; "us" and "them".[24] Simplistic generalizations of this sort obscure the complexities of development and ignore the evidence – for instance, that tradition and modernity coexist in most societies, often without well-defined distinctions; that there are varied conceptions of what constitutes development; and that apparently dissimilar values in different societies may complement each other.

It is one thing to believe and practice our faith, it is another thing to really go down to the ground and see how our faith can be translated into use for people who are asking for help.[23]

Such labelling falls into the trap of using the observers' own value systems and norms to interpret the ways of life in other societies. It may overlook some cultures entirely, particularly those considered inferior or backward. It may assign labels in very general terms and with little attention to cultural variety. For example, assuming that women in all non-Western societies are subject to male oppression[25] is more than an egregious theoretical error; in practical terms it overlooks the power and agency that both men and women may exercise as guardians of cultural values.

Similar crude categorizations lead to the false and dangerous assumption that all people accept all the cultural values of their own societies. People who share the same culture can and do disagree about values, customs, norms, objectives and courses of action. These disagreements can give rise to various forms of internal resistance, which then encourage transitions from within. For example, movements against gender inequalities in faith groups have come from within the groups, from both women and men.[26] Male advocacy against gender inequalities is an effective mechanism for cultural change.

The challenge for UNFPA is to help countries as we always have, with no agenda of our own; with sensitivity towards unique cultural values; with an infinite willingness to work with whatever is positive; and with a determination to help countries and people turn universal principles into concrete action.

—Thoraya Ahmed Obaid, Executive Director, UNFPA

A discussion that starts with assumptions about "values" may end with moral relativism in which appeals for cultural sensitivity and engagement are interpreted as acceptance that all values and cultural practices are equally significant. Moral relativism provides no basis for action because all local values and practices are considered equally valid. The result in development terms is stalemate and frustration.

Cultural awareness and sensitivity do not imply moral relativism. Finding out what people believe and think, finding out what makes sense to people and working with that knowledge does not require equal acceptance of all values and practices. Values and practices that infringe upon human rights can be found in all cultures. The practical course is not to avoid cultural engagement but to embrace it; culturally sensitive approaches can reveal the most effective ways of challenging harmful cultural practices and strengthening positive ones.

Why Are Culturally Sensitive Approaches Critical?

Culturally sensitive approaches are an obligation for organizations and people concerned about human development. They are also a "logical and practical imperative"[27] for successful development, for the following key reasons:

First, people have a human right to have their cultural knowledge and interests included in the development policies and programmes that concern them. This is consistent with the Declaration on the Right to Development adopted through General Assembly resolution 41/128 on December 4, 1986.[28] In the preamble, the General Assembly expressed concern:

> …*at the existence of serious obstacles to development, as well as to the complete fulfilment of human beings and of peoples, constituted,* inter alia, *by the denial of civil, political, economic, social and cultural rights, and considering that all human rights and fundamental freedoms are indivisible and interdependent and that, in order to promote development, equal attention and urgent consideration should be given to the implementation, promotion and protection of civil, political, economic, social and cultural rights and that, accordingly, the promotion of, respect for and enjoyment of certain human rights and fundamental freedoms*

A well-meaning outsider's best intentions to provide aid will be futile if none of his or her priorities correspond with those of the person being helped nor engage with his or her culture and political or economic institutions. It is all too easy and too human to forget that there are also the good intentions of a local welfare mechanism that existed well before the invention of … assistance, and a humane value system that does not depend on outsiders to tell people to take care of their weakest members.[29]

cannot justify the denial of other human rights and fundamental freedoms….

ARTICLE 1 OF THE DECLARATION STATES:

The right to development is an inalienable human right by virtue of which every human person and all peoples are entitled to participate in, contribute to, and enjoy economic, social, cultural and political development, in which all human rights and fundamental freedoms can be fully realized.

ARTICLE 2 STATES:

The human person is the central subject of development and should be the active participant and beneficiary of the right to development….All human beings have a responsibility for development, individually and collectively, taking into account the need for full respect for their human rights and fundamental freedoms as well as their duties to the community, which alone can ensure the free and complete fulfilment of the human being, and they should therefore promote and protect an appropriate political, social and economic order for development.

Second, culturally sensitive approaches uncover the creative solutions that abound within cultures. Conversely, wholesale dismissal and lack of serious regard for cultures overlook the "indigenous … customs and traditional practices [that] can contribute positively to development planning".[30]

Third, culturally sensitive approaches are crucial for understanding local contexts. This is important, since development programmes can succeed only by being relevant to the cultural environments in which they are implemented.[31]

Fourth, cultural knowledge is indispensable for understanding power relationships in cultural groups and the implications for development policies. Cultural awareness of this sort dispenses with generalizations. It recognizes that women and men, boys and girls are not homogenous groups; there are stratifications with respect to race, class, age, language, ethnicity, among other variables, which can lead to different development processes and outcomes.

Fifth, it is only with culturally sensitive approaches that it is possible to begin to address rigid and harmful ethnocentrisms within development. People inevitably label others, based in large part on their own cultural frameworks. If development organizations and actors are not explicit to themselves about how they understand culture, then they will make implicit and possibly unhelpful assumptions about culture in what they do.

To see ourselves as others see us can be eye-opening. To see others as sharing a nature with ourselves is merest decency. But it is from the far more difficult achievement of seeing ourselves amongst others, as a local example of the forms human life has locally taken, a case among cases, a world among worlds, that the largeness of mind – without which objectivity is self-congratulation and tolerance a sham – comes.[32]

Overview of the Chapters

This report demonstrates why and how culturally sensitive approaches matter for development processes and outcomes. Each chapter focuses on a selected priority area for the ICPD and MDGs: human rights and gender relations, gender equality, reproductive rights and health, population dynamics and conflict.

CHAPTER 2: Negotiating Culture: Building Support for Human Rights

This chapter revisits debates on the universality of the human rights framework, as well as arguments about the inherent opposition of human rights and culture. It notes the "difficulties of drawing sharp distinctions between

---

3 THE CULTURE LENS

The culture lens is UNFPA's tool for easing the process of contesting and changing the practices that underpin gender inequality and for building the alliances that will promote programme effectiveness and ownership. It also helps to develop the skills – the cultural fluency – needed for negotiating with individuals, groups and communities, for persuading stakeholders and partners, and for cultivating cultural acceptance and ownership of gender equity, gender equality and human rights.

The culture lens helps to:

- understand the needs and aspirations of different groups, including the community's most marginalized members;
- conduct research to clarify political, social, legal and economic realities, as well as the possibilities for change;
- study community beliefs and practices and identify those most supportive of human rights, women's empowerment and gender equality;
- understand the politics among potential partners, such as pressure groups and civil society groups, and the politics required to build effective alliances;
- learn the cultural language – develop "cultural fluency" – which will be necessary to learn, negotiate and persuade;
- establish connections between local cultural values and universally recognized human rights; and
- develop the communication, mediation, negotiation and facilitation skills needed to build trust, resolve conflicts and encourage ownership of human rights and gender equality.

HUMAN RIGHTS & GENDER EQUITY AND EQUALITY

KNOWLEDGE
- Local Pressure Groups and Power Structures
- Community Needs and Aspirations
- Community Acceptance and Ownership
- Political, Legal, Social, Culture and Economic Realities

SKILLS
- Communication Mediation/Negotiation and Facilitation Skills
- Language Sensitivity to Culturally Specific Contexts

Source: UNFPA. 2008. *Integrating Culture, Gender and Human Rights in Programming: A Training Manual.* New York. UNFPA.

▲ *Woman carries heavy load in the countryside of Nepal.*
© Peter Bruyneel

culture and human rights or seeing relativism and universalism as diametrically opposed and incompatible situations".[33] The chapter underscores that cultural awareness and sensitivity do **not** mean moral relativism. Indeed, the advantage of culturally sensitive approaches is that they provide insights on how to align cultural practices and human rights most effectively. Culturally sensitive approaches are critical for building cultural support for human rights: "Culture is the context within which human rights have to be specified and realized."[34] The chapter outlines how culturally sensitive approaches can help to build cultural legitimacy for human rights.

CHAPTER 3: Negotiating Culture: Promoting Gender Equality and Empowering Women

Chapter 3 argues that culturally sensitive approaches are important for promoting gender equality and empowering women. Using case examples, the chapter describes the analytical approaches and programming strategies that have worked well in different contexts. It highlights the importance of a gendered approach that studies the expe-

riences of men, women, boys and girls in different social contexts and that focuses on understanding the ways in which variables such as class, race, ethnicity, faith and age cut across gender and affect people's experiences of rights and culture. The chapter emphasizes that culturally sensitive approaches are not only concerned with **what** meanings are significant, but in order to understand diversities, they must also unravel **why** these meanings are significant. Cultural approaches that are sensitive to power must be interested in who holds those meanings in common, through what processes and with what effects. This depth of knowledge is important for forming partnerships and for building on existing local actions.

CHAPTER 4: Negotiating Culture: Reproductive Health and Reproductive Rights

This chapter deepens the themes that were raised in chapter 3. It shows that disaggregated and politically sensitive cultural approaches are essential for dealing with reproductive health and reproductive rights. Using case reports, the chapter highlights the importance of understanding contexts: Cultural insights illuminate how context influences individual reproductive choices. In turn, this structures the kinds of interventions needed to accommodate mindsets and behavioural patterns. This is part of the value of culturally sensitive approaches. Like chapter 3, this chapter also demonstrates how a gendered approach that is sensitive to "intersectionalities" such as class, race, ethnicity, faith and age is critical for negotiating cultures and securing reproductive rights and reproductive health.

CHAPTER 5: Negotiating Culture: Poverty, Inequality and Population

Chapter 5 discusses cultural questions in the context of poverty and inequality. The chapter points out that development strategies commonly exclude about 750 million members of cultural minorities; discusses the consequences for health, well-being, women's empowerment and gender equality; and gives some examples of successful approaches.

CHAPTER 6: Negotiating Culture: Gender and Reproductive Health in Conflict Situations

This chapter uses case examples to show how and why culturally sensitive approaches are critical for promoting gender equality and empowering women in the context of war. Again, the examples reinforce themes that were raised in earlier chapters, including the importance of a gendered approach and the need to be aware of intersectionalities. The chapter describes analytical approaches and suggests practical strategies for implementing culturally sensitive approaches.

CHAPTER 7: Negotiating Culture: Some Conclusions

This chapter pulls together the threads of the report, and offers some suggestions for action.

2 Negotiating Culture: Building Support for Human Rights

Legitimating human rights in local cultures and religious traditions is a matter of vital importance for the survival and future development of the human rights paradigm itself.[1]

The United Nations Charter (1945) included respect for human rights among its key purposes:

> *The purposes of the United Nations are … to achieve international cooperation in solving international problems of an economic, social, cultural or humanitarian character, and in promoting and encouraging respect for human rights and for fundamental freedoms for all without distinction as to race, sex, language or religion.*[2]

A broad consensus developed during the early days of the United Nations that, in response to "barbarous acts which have outraged the conscience of mankind",[3] a further statement was needed enumerating the fundamental rights shared by all human beings without distinction. These rights were to be more than theoretical; the aim was to put an end to the brutality and suffering seen in the 1930s and 1940s.

The subsequent Universal Declaration of Human Rights (1948) outlined the human rights paradigm:

> *The Universal Declaration of Human Rights underlines the rights of all human beings to life, liberty and security of person (Article 3); to freedom from slavery or servitude (Article 4); to freedom from torture or cruel, inhumane or degrading treatment or punishment (Article 5); to recognition and equality before the law (Articles 6 and 7); to effective and fair redress before the law (Articles 8-12); to freedom of movement (Article 13) and freedom to seek asylum from persecution, except where the individual is being prosecuted for non-political crimes (Article 14); to a nationality and to change nationalities (Article 15); to marry and to have a family, with free and full consent of the spouses (Article 16); to own property individually (Article 17); to freedom of thought, conscience and religion,*

◀ *An elderly woman discusses her treatment with a health care provider. Human rights, including the right to health, are universal and indivisible across age, gender and culture.*
© Peter Bruyneel

to change religion or belief and to practise religion (Article 18); to freedom of opinion, expression and dissemination of ideas without interference (Article 19); to assemble peacefully (Article 20); to participate in government (Article 21); to social security and economic, social and cultural rights which are indispensable for dignity (Article 22); to work in a chosen occupation without fear of discrimination and under equal conditions (Article 23); to rest and enjoy periodic holidays with pay (Article 24); to a standard of living adequate for health and well-being (Article 25); to education, which should be free in the foundational stages (Article 26); to participation in cultural life (Article 27) and to "a social and international order in which the rights and freedoms set forth in this Declaration can be fully realized" (Article 28).[4]

The Declaration is a "common standard of achievement for all peoples and all nations".[5] It has both moral and legal force. Member States of the United Nations have also ratified a wide range of instruments on specific aspects of human rights that, once they have entered into force, are binding under international law. Certain norms, including the prohibition of crimes against humanity, genocide and war crimes, apply to all States, whether they are signatories or not.

Various human rights instruments have established international legal standards. These include the conventions on genocide (1948), slavery (1956), labour rights (1966), the rights of the child (Convention on the Rights of the Child [CRC] 1989), and elimination of discrimination on grounds of race (1965) and gender (the Convention on the Elimination of All Forms of Discrimination against Women [CEDAW] 1979). The Geneva Conventions (1949) and the Refugees Convention (1951) outline humanitarian principles applicable in situations of conflict.

These treaties and conventions elaborate on the core human rights principles of universality, indivisibility, interdependence, equality and non-discrimination. In addition, the International Covenant on Economic, Social and Cultural Rights (1966) and other major consensus documents from the World Conference on Human Rights (1993), the International Conference on Population and Development (1994) and the Fourth World Conference on Women, Beijing (1995), elaborate clear human rights principles.

Ratification of human rights instruments by a sovereign State does not necessarily indicate full compliance; neither does it mean that all the State's citizens are convinced that the agreed principles can be applied within their particular cultural contexts. Nevertheless, States agree to be bound by the human rights instruments they have ratified. An instrument comes into force once an agreed number of Member States have ratified it.

The Debate Over Human Rights

One of the lasting controversies surrounding the Universal Declaration of Human Rights concerns the extent to which the rights referred to are in fact universal. One line of argument asserts that the human rights framework cannot present a universal position, for a number of reasons. First, the original Declaration was ratified by the select group of principally European countries represented in the United Nations in 1948 – some of the very countries that proclaimed the universality of the Declaration were still maintaining colonies at that time. Second, these countries drafted the Declaration based on their own cultural assumptions, constitutional experiences and political struggles, e.g., to separate religion and state. According to this view, the human rights framework reflects "Western" cultures and values and pays little attention to other cultures' assumptions and experiences. For example, the emphasis on individual rights to property reflects a concept of ownership which was far from universal before the colonial period. This view holds that the framework "downplays the importance of community … [and] seeks to impose an individual model of rights that is at odds with non-Western ways of life".[6] Again, many developing countries have not had the political struggle over "church and state" that occurred in Europe and the United States, and there is sometimes considerable resistance to locating religion solely in the private realm.[7]

Such arguments have been heard in both developed and developing countries. In 1947, even before the Declaration could be adopted, the American Anthropological Association challenged its universality:

How can the proposed Declaration be applicable to all human beings and not be a statement of rights conceived only in terms of the values prevalent in the countries of Western Europe and America? … Standards and values are relative to the culture from which they derive so that any attempt to formulate postulates that grow out of the beliefs and moral codes of one culture must to that extent detract from the applicability of any Declaration of Human Rights to mankind as a whole.[8]

Given these concerns, some opponents of the universalist position call for a multicultural approach to building and adapting the human rights framework, possibly including the processes required to adjudicate human rights. While the Declaration relies on formal legal State mechanisms, as in European models, some developing countries emphasize the efficiency and effectiveness of their customary norms and procedures, including religious ones. (Some legal scholars recognize the practicality of this approach, arguing that the costs of accessing the legal system are often prohibitive for ordinary men and women and that customary procedures appropriately aligned with human rights would provide more immediate access.) Others reject particular human rights provisions on cultural grounds. Some of the most acrimonious contestations over the universality of the human rights framework concern

Where, after all, do universal human rights begin? In small places, close to home – so close and so small that they cannot be seen on any maps of the world. Yet they are the world of individual persons, the neighbourhood they live in, the school they attend, the factory, farm or office they work in. Such are the places where every man, woman or child seeks equal justice, equal opportunities, and equal dignity without discrimination. Unless these rights have meaning there, they have little meaning anywhere.

—Eleanor Roosevelt

conventions perceived as undermining cultural and religious norms on family and gender relations. Other reservations are based on political, legal or constitutional grounds.

The Evolving Nature of Human Rights

Analysts have described the ways in which the human rights framework has progressed over the last 60 years and the roles of cultures in promoting it. Membership in the United Nations has expanded to include as sovereign States nearly all former colonies. Since 1948, human rights have become less individualized. They have moved beyond protecting individuals within States and now include protections for the collective rights of groups, such as indigenous peoples, minorities and emerging nations. The framework now includes provisions for economic, social and cultural rights. Rights such as the right to reproductive health, and to be free from gender-based violence, have been elaborated. In 1993 – 45 years after the Universal Declaration of Human Rights was adopted, and 12 years after CEDAW entered into force – 171 nations at the World Conference on Human Rights in Vienna confirmed that women's rights were human rights. Also in 1993, the United Nations adopted the Declaration on the Elimination of Violence, which led to the inclusion of a section on gender-based violence at the 1994 International Conference on Population and Development (ICPD) held in Cairo, during which 179 governments acknowledged reproductive health as part of the overall right to health, and to the World Conference on Women at Beijing in 1995. The process demonstrates the ability of the international human rights framework to recognize cultural change as it is taking place:

Understanding culture as fixed, uniform and unchanging ignores the impacts of globalization in the present and historical transfers of cultural beliefs and practices in the past. Considering cultures as changing and interconnected, and rights as historically created and transnationally redefined by national and local actors, better describes the contemporary situation. It also describes the impossibility of drawing sharp distinctions between culture and rights or seeing relativism and universalism as diametrically opposed and incompatible situations.[9]

As the framework has evolved, the language and politics of human rights have opened space for cultural changes. People are using the language of rights to make their own claims. This is because the language of rights is the language of resistance to deprivation and oppression, which is common to all cultures. "Viewed from this perspective, human rights are both universal and particular: universal because the experience of resistance to oppression is shared among subjugated groups the world over, but also particular because resistance is shaped in response to the peculiarities of the relevant social context."[10] This reaffirms the importance of understanding rights within their contexts; in other words, the need for culturally sensitive approaches to promoting human rights.

Culturally sensitive approaches recognize that:
- People across cultures understand rights in different ways.
- People within cultures also have different perspectives on and experiences of rights.
- People within and across cultures advocate for rights in ways that suit their contexts.
- Human rights can be ingrained through "cultural legitimacy".
- Facilitating cultural legitimacy requires cultural knowledge and engagement.

How can one aspire to achieve progress and prosperity while women, who make up half the society, experience a long-standing neglect of their interests and the rights granted to them by our religion that put them on the same footing with men? These rights voice women's noble mission and grant them justice over the inequity and violence that may befall them, despite the fact that they have made equal achievements to men, in both education and employment."[11]

Go to the people. Live with them. Learn from them. Love them. Start with what they know. Build with what they love. With the best leaders, when the work is done, the task accomplished, the people will say: "We have done this ourselves!"[12]

Culture absolutely does not sit still. Any presumption of immutability – explicit or implicit – can be disastrously deceptive. To talk of, say, the Hindu culture, or for that matter the Indian culture, taken to be well-defined and historically unaltered, not only overlooks the great variations within each of these categories, but also ignores their evolution and their large variations over time.[13]

Building Cultural Legitimacy for Human Rights

Culturally sensitive approaches are action-oriented. They can provide effective tools for understanding the interrelationships between human rights and cultures, as well as for tackling oppression within cultures. Culturally sensitive approaches recognize that "people are more likely to observe normative propositions if they believe them to be sanctioned by their own cultural traditions" and that "observance of human rights standards [relies] on cultural legitimacy".[14] However, the processes for encouraging this cultural legitimacy require important safeguards:

- *The approach to engaging with culture must itself be guided by human rights principles of non-discrimination, equality and accountability.* Taken seriously, these principles can improve the prospect that people will be treated with respect and dignity. Human rights principles put a check on the rigid ethnocentricity that regard all "other" cultures as inferior and as having little or nothing to contribute to development thinking and processes. The danger of imposing particular interpretations of rights is that such interpretations undermine cultural ownership and can culminate in resistance and resentment: "Even though outsiders may sympathize with and wish to support the dominated and oppressed groups or classes, their claiming to know … the valid view of the culture of that society will

▲ *A strong civil society is important for promoting human rights. Young women in training as health aides with help from an NGO.*
© UNFPA

not accomplish this effectively...."[17] This does not mean that all cultural norms and practices should be accepted and tolerated. However, culturally sensitive approaches encourage "cross-cultural moral judgment and action" and also point to "the best ways of formu-

> *In intercultural relations, morality and knowledge cannot be the exclusive product of some cultures but not of others.*[15]

lating judgment and of undertaking action".[18]

- *The practical starting point to building the rights and freedoms necessary for human development is not to avoid the struggles over the meanings of rights, but to acknowledge them; that is, to find out where they are located and the perspectives and roles of different actors.* Culturally sensitive approaches must then locate their conversations within those contexts. UNFPA, United Nations Population Fund, has learned the importance of identifying and working with local actors committed to change in order to support locally owned initiatives for advancing human rights. The organization has developed partnerships with parliamentarians, media and civil society organizations (including those that address

human rights and women's issues), influential faith- and inter-faith-based organizations, and local power structures such as community leaders. However, it also acknowledges the need for caution. It is keen to ensure that its partnerships do not obstruct cultural change nor prevent collective action among less organized and less powerful actors. In Benin, for example, UNFPA has been supporting Islamic institutions committed to improving women's rights. In the Occupied Palestinian Territory, it has been working with the Department of Family Counselling and Reconciliation in Shari'a Courts in order to address gender inequalities, gender-based violence and reproductive health and rights. In Tajikistan, UNFPA works with the Islamic University of Tajikistan, the Government's Religious Committee and the non-governmental organization Safe Motherhood on issues such as reproductive health and rights and gender equality. In Jamaica, UNFPA

> *The world over, people generally think that they perceive reality and approach problem-solving in a way that is objective, accurate and value- or culture-free. In fact, the way in which we interpret evidence depends very much on our own individual cultural context.*[16]

In our work around the world, we have found that building alliances with and involving members of religious traditions can actually determine a programme's success or failure....[19]

works with the United Theological School of the West Indies to deal with issues including gender-based violence and HIV prevention and treatment. Regardless of location, UNFPA develops partnerships with institutions that have substantial influence within communities and are able to reach people and encourage change.[20]

- *Culturally sensitive approaches should contribute to policies by taking local norms and practices seriously into account.* This means working with and building on norms and practices that are supportive of core goals such as human rights, and subjecting those that are not to scrutiny and debate. "The practice of human rights risks losing relevance and legitimacy if it does not concern itself with what goes on at the local level."[21]

For example, in addressing what appears to be cultural legitimization of gender inequalities, some analysts argue that women's human rights activists should abandon approaches that "simply call for an end to cultural practices that contravene human rights principles". The contention is that such "abolitionist" approaches fail to understand the real contexts for these cultural attitudes and assume that women have no possibilities, avenues or resources to realize their rights. These approaches start from the position that the only viable solutions are those proposed in formal national and international human rights legislations.

However, state and local institutions do influence cultural change; local institutions are sometimes the most accessible and affordable recourse for people who live in rural areas, and customary systems can recognize claims not cited in formal laws. While it is true that cultural institutions can present substantial obstacles – particularly where there is a lack of knowledge of options, where gender roles are firmly entrenched within families and where women's participation in decision-making is circumscribed – there are variations within cultures.

---

4 INDIA: ADDRESSING THE SEX-RATIO BALANCE

There are substantial family and social pressures to produce sons in India and there is widespread discrimination against girls. Some regions continue to practice female infanticide, but new technologies for sex selection may now be making the more substantial contribution to declining sex ratios.

In 1986, following intense advocacy from health and human rights activists, the Indian State of Maharashtra passed laws to ban the use of prenatal diagnostic techniques for sex selection. Later, campaigns at the national level resulted in the 1994 Prenatal Diagnostics Techniques (Regulation and Prevention of Misuse) Act. However, sex selection continued, so, in 2000, health activists went to the Supreme Court to demand enforcement of the legislation. Meanwhile, various United Nations organizations, including UNFPA, UNICEF and WHO, were working with international non-governmental organizations (NGOs) and India's Ministry of Health and Family Welfare to engage the media, build networks and provide training and support for local groups, including faith-based organizations, committed to ending sex selection. This comprehensive approach has begun to change perceptions and attitudes. While the practice has not been entirely eradicated, there has been notable progress. Changing harmful practices requires more than legal action; it depends on collaboration and integrated actions across a broad range of actors at national and local levels.

Source: Adapted from http://www.unfpa.org/culture/case_studies/india_study.htm. Accessed March 2008

- *Culturally sensitive approaches must not only explore and engage with local systems of meanings but also understand cultures at national and international levels and recognize the interrelationships among them.* An intimate understanding of the ongoing conversations among national, local and international actors and agencies can reveal both the paths and obstacles to action, as well as the appropriate methods and strategies for engagement. UNFPA, the United Nations Children's Fund (UNICEF) and the World Health Organization (WHO) found that this multi-pronged strategy was important for working with international, national and local human rights advocates in tackling sex selection in India (see Box 4).

- *Culturally sensitive approaches must be gendered.* Gender analysis is important for understanding how different categories of men and women, boys and girls experience rights.

> *A gendered approach to rights fundamentally shifts the way that rights are understood. It requires understanding rights not merely as legal entitlements but also as a political tool in social change strategies. Combining gender and rights provides a way to examine values, behaviours, assumptions, policies and programme decisions to determine how they play a role in excluding or discriminating against some people and favouring others; and looking at different kinds of subordination, based on gender as well as class, ethnicity, caste, age and other factors. Essentially, a gendered analysis of rights reminds us that rights do not apply to some neutral individual, but rather the application and enjoyment of rights differs according to a person's power and position in society and the roles that are attributed to her or him.*[22]

With this understanding, culturally sensitive approaches are important for building support for human rights and gender equality deep within local and national contexts. Culturally sensitive approaches focus on the intimate, core areas where human rights are rooted, recognizing that in order for human rights to be sustained, they have to be internalized.

> *The objective is to build ownership of the human rights agenda within communities. The goal is the achievement of human rights and gender equality. The strategy is to work from within communities and cultures to build a broad base for human rights and gender equality. For UNFPA, the human rights-based approach, gender mainstreaming and culturally sensitive approaches go hand in hand to maximize the chance of success.*[23]

In order to build cultural legitimacy for human rights, culturally sensitive approaches must include all societies and reach into communities. This process should over time build ownership for human rights. Culturally sensitive

> *Contrary to what some may claim or fear, such an engagement with culture does not erode or deform local culture but rather challenges its discriminatory and oppressive aspects. This of course may provoke resistance from those who have a vested interest in preserving the status quo. Negotiating culture with human rights concerns inherently questions, [delegitimizes], destabilizes, ruptures and, in the long run, destroys oppressive hierarchies. It also contributes to harnessing the positive elements of local culture to advance human rights and gender equality, a process that also revalidates the culture itself....*[24]

approaches must go beyond this and reach marginalized groups within communities so that these groups will have a determining voice in their own cultures and be able fully to exercise their human rights. In many communities, the most marginalized and oppressed groups are women and children. Certain categories – particular classes, ethnic groups, religions, cultures – can suffer worse forms of discrimination and oppression.

Culturally sensitive approaches cannot promise immediate and predictable results. Development is complex, and cultural issues are among the most sensitive to tackle. Yet, changes fundamental to human development, which require full realization of human rights, invariably depend on serious and respectful engagement with cultures.

3 Negotiating Culture: Promoting Gender Equality and Empowering Women[1]

Cultures are neither static nor monolithic…. They adapt to new opportunities and challenges and evolving realities. What is seen as "the culture" may in fact be a viewpoint held by a small group of elites keen to hold onto their power and status. The tensions and diverging goals inherent in every culture create opportunities for UNFPA to promote human rights and gender equality, particularly when UNFPA can partner with local agents of social change and challenge dominant views from within the same cultural frame of reference.[2]

At the first United Nations World Conference on Women in Mexico City in 1975, governments, civil society and United Nations bodies committed themselves to work with and for women. Work continued throughout the United Nations Decade for Women, 1976 to 1985. The United Nations General Assembly adopted the Convention on the Elimination of All Forms of Discrimination against Women (CEDAW) in 1979. CEDAW established an agenda for national action to end discrimination and promote equality between men and women. It defined discrimination as "any distinction, exclusion or restriction made on the basis of sex which has the effect or purpose of impairing or nullifying the recognition, enjoyment or exercise by women, irrespective of their marital status, on a basis of equality of men and women, of human rights and fundamental freedoms in the political, economic, social, cultural, civil or any other field."

Equality between women and men was one of the major themes of subsequent World Conferences on Women. The Beijing Declaration and Platform for Action (1995) explicitly linked gender equality with women's empowerment:

Women's empowerment and their full participation on the basis of equality in all spheres of society, including participation in the decision-making process and access to power, are fundamental for the achievement of equality, development and peace.

◀ *As cultures change, gender roles, responsibilities and relationships change too. This young man in Côte d'Ivoire is learning to sew in a mixed class of women and men.*
© Jane Hahn/Panos

The Beijing Platform for Action maintains that similarities and differences between women and men should be recognized and equally valued, and that women and men should enjoy equal status; recognition and consideration; equal conditions "to realize their full potential and ambitions"; equal "opportunities to participate in, contribute to, and benefit from society's resources and development"; equal "freedoms and quality of life"; and equal "outcomes in all aspects of life".[3]

> *Gender equality is, first and foremost, a human right. Women are entitled to live in dignity and in freedom from want and from fear. Empowering women is also an indispensable tool for advancing development and reducing poverty.*[4]

For Beijing+5 in June 2000, governments – with involvement from the United Nations, non-governmental organizations (NGOs) and regional organizations – reviewed progress on women's empowerment and gender equality since 1995. National reports found significant changes in the status of women since 1976; for example, more women were involved in the labour force and were major actors in civil society. Governments credited NGOs and women's organizations with advancing concerns about women and gender equality. However, reports from all regions also noted that violence and poverty compromised gender equality. Globalization presented new challenges, with increasing "trafficking in women and girls, the changing nature of armed conflict, the growing gap between nations and genders, and the detachment of macroeconomic policy from social protection concerns". Women still had limited presence and power in political structures at both national and international levels. It was important to ensure "more careful monitoring of progress in ensuring women's equal participation in these positions of economic power".[5]

Beijing+5 outlined plans for future actions, which included:
- gender mainstreaming in all areas and at all levels and the complementarity between mainstreaming and special activities targeting women;

5 SELECTED FACTS ON GENDER EQUALITY

- Of the world's one billion poorest people, three fifths are women and girls.
- Of the 960 million adults in the world who cannot read, two thirds are women.
- Seventy per cent of the 130 million children who are out of school are girls.
- With notable exceptions, such as Rwanda and the Nordic countries, women are conspicuously absent from parliaments, making up, on average, only 16 per cent of parliamentarians worldwide.
- Everywhere, women typically earn less than men, both because they are concentrated in low-paying jobs and because they are paid less for the same work.
- Although women spend about 70 per cent of their unpaid time caring for family members, that contribution to the global economy remains invisible.
- Up to half of all adult women have experienced violence at the hands of their intimate partners.
- Systematic sexual violence against women has characterized almost all recent armed conflicts and is used as a tool of terror and "ethnic cleansing".
- In sub-Saharan Africa, 57 per cent of those living with HIV are women, and young women aged 15 to 24 years are at least three times more likely to be infected than men of the same age.
- Each year, half a million women die and 10 to 15 million suffer chronic disability from preventable complications of pregnancy and childbirth.

Source: UNDP. 2006. *Taking Gender Equality Seriously: Making Progress, Meeting New Challenges.* New York. UNDP: 2006. http://www.undp.org.pl/publikacje/TakingGenderEqualitySeriously.pdf, accessed June 2008.

- special focus on education, social services and health, including sexual and reproductive health;
- the HIV and AIDS pandemic;
- violence against women and girls;
- the persistent and increasing burden of poverty on women;
- vulnerability of migrant women including exploitation and trafficking;
- natural disaster and environmental management;
- development of strong, effective and accessible national machineries for the advancement of women;
- formulation of strategies to enable women and men to reconcile and share equally work and family responsibilities; and

- women's access to decision-making, particularly in peacekeeping processes.

Specific targets were established and others were confirmed, such as:

- closing the gender gap in primary and secondary education by 2005, and free, compulsory and universal primary education for both girls and boys by 2015;
- achieving a 50 per cent improvement in levels of adult literacy by 2015, especially for women;
- creating and maintaining a non-discriminatory, as well as gender-sensitive, legal environment through reviewing legislation with a view to striving to remove discriminatory provisions as soon as possible, preferably by 2005;
- providing universal access to high quality primary health care throughout the life cycle, including sexual and reproductive health care, not later than 2015.[6]

In its 2005 review, Beijing+10 noted significant progress in promoting awareness of gender equality among governments and the public, including greater knowledge of how globalization, market liberalization, privatization, migration and the use of new technologies affect women. Improvements were noted in child and maternal mortality and education and literacy for women and girls. Issues such as the effects on girls and women of HIV and AIDS, trafficking and gender-based violence were also receiving greater attention. At the policy level, the importance of gender mainstreaming and of effective linkages and complementarities across policies, legislation and programming were also taking root. However, there was still a need for more multidimensional strategies that would bridge the gap between policies and practice. Furthermore, despite the policy and institutional changes, gender stereotypes were still pervasive and resulted in discriminatory practices.[7]

The Beijing Platform For Action and the subsequent amendments in Beijing+5 and Beijing+10 provide the framework for the Millennium Development Goals (MDGs), 2000, which recognize that "the promotion of gender equality and the empowerment of women are critical to the eradication of poverty, hunger and disease and the achievement of development that is truly sustainable".[8] Goal 3 is dedicated to the promotion of gender equality and the empowerment of women. It has been noted that all the other goals require a gender perspective, and there is a call to incorporate gender throughout the implementation of the MDGs. The Beijing Platform for Action also provides a framework for implementing the Programme of Action of the International Conference on Population and Development (ICPD), with programmes for gender equality in areas of reproductive health care, education and literacy, unmet need for contraception, maternal mortality and morbidity reduction and HIV and AIDS.

What culture worth the name would deny women the right to safe motherhood? What value system would send young people ignorant into the world, when a little knowledge might save their lives?

—Dr. Nafis Sadik, UNFPA Executive Director, 1987-2000

Gender Equality, Women's Empowerment and Culture

"Cultural issues are behind the observed differentials between men and women in terms of participation in the different spheres of development," says a report by UNFPA, United Nations Population Fund, on cultural programming in Asia.[9] Reports from Beijing+5 and Beijing+10 emphasized that stubborn cultural stereotypes of women persist despite institutional and policy changes.

Deep-rooted cultural beliefs sustain gender inequality. In Latin America, for example, feminist movements against domestic violence have found that cultural traditions that support patriarchal violence are among the major impediments to change. French, Spanish and Portuguese colonies followed the Code Napoleon, under which the father or husband had total power over the family and could treat them as he saw fit.[10] The tradition continued essentially unchallenged after independence and until recent times, as the struggle to enforce the Maria da Penha law in Brazil illustrates (see page 32).

POWER CAN BE:

- **Overt and Coercive**
  The more powerful can use their positions to compel others to act in ways they would prefer not to.

- **Hidden and Coercive**
  The more powerful can operate effectively from behind the scenes. For example, legal institutions may enforce social norms that discriminate against women and compel them to conform.

- **Overt and Non-Coercive**
  People may use power in non-conflictual and non-coercive ways, building agreements in order to achieve desired outcomes.

- **Hidden and Non-Coercive**
  Where there is tacit consensus, power relations are upheld unintentionally and even unconsciously. For example, there are groups which not only come to accept disadvantageous hierarchical arrangements but actively defend and uphold them.

Source: Moncrieffe, J. 2005. "Beyond Categories: Power, Recognition and the Conditions for Equity." Background paper for the *World Development Report 2006: Equity And Development.* New York: The World Bank.

Gender-based violence "is perpetuated through social and cultural norms and traditions, reinforcing male-dominated power structures".[11] From early infancy, women are taught "that they are inferior to men and often to blame for the violence inflicted upon them. As wives or partners, they must hold the family together, at any cost. Women and men both learn to turn a blind eye to, or accept, gender-based violence". Under these circumstances, domestic violence becomes "naturalized" and invisible.

Reports from Uganda demonstrate the ways in which cultures sustain unequal gender relations. Many men were adamant that their women are not supposed to have money: "After selling the maize, the husband may buy a dress or *lesu* for the wife. If women are allowed to own property, they will be on top of men." Women themselves provided a number of examples of the problems that occur when they were "allowed" to own property, particularly the difficulty of "sustaining a husband and economic independence; one has to be foregone".[12]

While beliefs may be changing among younger women, some older women retain and try to enforce them. In one area, the Uganda study found, women are forbidden from entering the lake. One younger woman asserted that there was nothing wrong with swimming in the lake. However, the older women objected. Women, they said, "should not go to the lake at all because they are always dirty". The "god" who was responsible for the site dictated this. Since the young women had failed to observe this instruction, the "god" would no longer bless the site.

Reports also show that domestic violence is widespread. "Husbands turn to battling their wives even on minor issues like failure to work hard in the garden or when his clothes are not washed (even if soap was not there)." It was reported that frustrated men were "beating their wives almost to death". Again, some women accepted and even justified this treatment: *It is us women who make the men beat us. Once the man goes to the lake, a woman gets another partner because she wants money. Women, especially the younger ones, have refused to stick to one partner. When there is a dance, all the men she has slept with gang up and beat her.*[13]

The Many Faces of Power: Examples from Africa

Power operates within cultures in many ways: through visible forms of coercion; hidden in legal norms, policies and governance structures;[14] and ingrained in the perceptions people have of themselves. People can internalize and project both positive and negative perceptions of who they are. Where women internalize negative perceptions, they may uphold harmful power relations unintentionally and even unconsciously. Women may not only come to accept disadvantageous hierarchical arrangements but actively defend and uphold them. It is within cultures that these perceptions, beliefs and systems of meaning are cultivated, internalized and sustained. It is also within cultures that power relations are transformed through contestation and consensus building in order to achieve desired outcomes.

The cultural challenges described above are common to Western and non-Western, developed and developing countries. For example, in Messobo, Ethiopia, the traditional practice of child marriage has resulted in multiple reproductive health complications, including obstetric fistula and maternal death. "The practice will only change when

Probably the most insidious of the three dimensions of power, invisible power shapes the psychological and ideological boundaries of participation. Significant problems and issues are not only kept from the decision-making table but also from the minds and consciousness of the different players involved, even those directly affected by the problem. By influencing how individuals think about their place in the world, this level of power shapes people's beliefs, sense of self and acceptance of the status quo – even their own superiority and inferiority.[16]

Ethiopian society begins to value women as equal players in the country's social and economic development."[15]

Popular culture and media in many societies treat women as sexual objects and present violence against women as normal. In some countries, representations of the "exotic woman" have more serious consequences for particular races. Gender inequalities – particularly for some categories of women and men – still exist, in both Western and non-Western societies.

Cultural Struggles Against Domestic Violence in Latin America

Advances in gender equality have never come without cultural struggles against the visible and invisible dimen-sions of power and the practices that sustain gender inequalities and oppress women.

Struggles to eradicate domestic violence have been going on throughout Latin America. Women's rights advocates have worked steadily and consistently for government legislation and effective public policies. They are also committed to eradicating the patriarchal values within cultural contexts that support gender-based violence, in order to place private violence in the public eye and "denaturalize" it. In 1994, the Organization of American States (OAS) adopted the Interamerican Convention to Prevent, Sanction and Eradicate Violence Against Women. Chile and Argentina adopted similar conventions in 1994; Bolivia, Ecuador and Panama in

7 **MAYMANA AND MOZIFUL'S STORY**

Maymana and her son Moziful live in a village just outside central Bangladesh. By Maymana's account, up to the early 1990s, she, her husband Hafeez and their three children were only occasion-ally poor, with a modest income and a few assets, including three rickshaws and an acre of paddy land. However, Hafeez fell ill. He visited the local phar-macist, who provided medicines but was not equipped to diagnose the problem. At the government health centre, staff requested bribes but did not treat him. A local doctor informed him that he need-ed special medicines. The rickshaws had to be sold to meet the medical expenses. The family reduced consumption and stopped purchasing small amenities.

Hafeez got progressively worse and eventually died, leaving Maymana and her son Moziful, then 12 years old, alone (by now both daughters were married). Following local custom, Maymana's father-in-law took control of the plot of land, which meant that Maymana had to resort to borrowing and begging for food. Moziful managed to find casual employ-ment, but he had a disability which brought stigma within the community.

Despite warnings and threats, Maymana decided to seek legal redress and brought her case against her father-in-law to the local village court. Though she had rights to the land according to Bangladeshi law, her claim was pre-dictably unsuccessful: The court followed traditional custom, which was biased against women, and allowed her father-in-law to retain ownership. As a result, Maymana and Moziful (both of whom are illiterate and ill) rely on social net-works for survival.

The community regards Maymana as "deserving poor" (a distressed woman) who, though in need of charity, is not entitled to full membership in the women's group. Charity, loans and Moziful's meagre earnings have allowed them to avoid destitution, though they subsist in chronic poverty. Socially ascribed identities—as reflected in atti-tudes to disability, old age, women, illness and misfortune—have entitled Maymana and Moziful to some assis-tance, but at the same time have blocked possible escape routes.

Source: From Hulme, D. 2003. "Thinking 'Small' and the Understanding of Poverty: Maymana And Mofizul's Story". Working Paper No 22. Manchester: Institute for Development Policy and Management.

1995; Colombia, Costa Rica, El Salvador, Guatemala, Nicaragua and Peru in 1996; and the Dominican Republic modified its penal code to include legislation against domestic violence in 1997.[18]

In Brazil, the process of change started with the creation of special police stations for battered women (*delegacias especiais de atendimento às mulheres,* or DEAMs), ideally staffed by policewomen. The first such police station was created in São Paulo in 1985 and there are now over 300 in the country. Many states have built reference centres and shelters for battered women, and provided a network of services to assist female victims of violence. However, the major instrument to combat domestic violence was developed fairly recently. Law no. 11.340, sanctioned on 7 August 2006, and named *Lei Maria da Penha* (in honour of a woman shot and crippled for life by her ex-companion 20 years ago),

not only increases the period of imprisonment for such violent acts from one to three years but it also allows preventive arrests and arrests for flagrant conduct. In addition, it includes a number of measures to protect the woman.

However, legislation to criminalize domestic violence is not always sufficient. In Brazil, several judges have claimed that the Maria da Penha law is "unconstitutional" because it "discriminates" against men. Some have called for women's submission, as in former times. Feminists recognize that engaging with culture is essential for eradicating domestic violence and that "cultural factors can … be harnessed to bring about change for the better".[19, 20]

> *The achievement of … gender equality in the West required and still requires a transformation of the cultures of many institutions – workplaces, trade unions, the church, professions, families, political parties, schools, etc. – all at a different rate and in different ways. Gender equality … could just as well have been described as alien to Western cultures as to non-Western ones. It was (and continues in important aspects to be), for example, rejected by the major Christian churches. It is the product of intense political struggle and cultural work, not immanence …. It is only in the last few decades that a wide gap has opened between the "West" and "non-West" on the issue of gender equality.*[17]

▲ *Guatemalan girl. Customs and traditions can be reassuring in times of change.*
© James Nelson/Getty Images

Culture, Gender and Human Rights

In cooperation with governments[21] and civil society organizations, UNFPA applies the principles outlined in United Nations instruments on gender equality and women's empowerment, which see gender equality as a human right and women's empowerment as critical for promoting human development. Its programming approach is firmly based in the ICPD Programme of Action, which requires "the establishment of common ground, with full respect for the various religious and ethical values and cultural backgrounds".[22] Culturally sensitive programming is key to building this common ground. It provides a practical and strategic response to the observation that cultural beliefs and perceptions are at the root of gender inequalities in many societies, and that gender equality and women's empowerment cannot be achieved unless they are also rooted in cultures.

> **8 PROMOTING GENDER EQUALITY AND EMPOWERING WOMEN: THE VALUE OF THE CULTURE LENS**
>
> UNFPA's cooperative approach to programming integrates three elements: human rights, gender main-streaming and cultural sensitivity. It is based on the following premises:
>
> - All human beings are entitled to equal rights and protections.
> - Gender mainstreaming is a strategic response to the widespread denial of women's human rights.
> - Culturally sensitive approaches involve communities in supporting human rights in many cultural contexts.
>
> **Source:** UNFPA. "Understanding Culture, Gender and Human Rights." http://unfpa.org/rights/main_presentation_3.swf, accessed June 2008. New York: UNFPA.

Figure 1: Understanding culture, gender and human rights

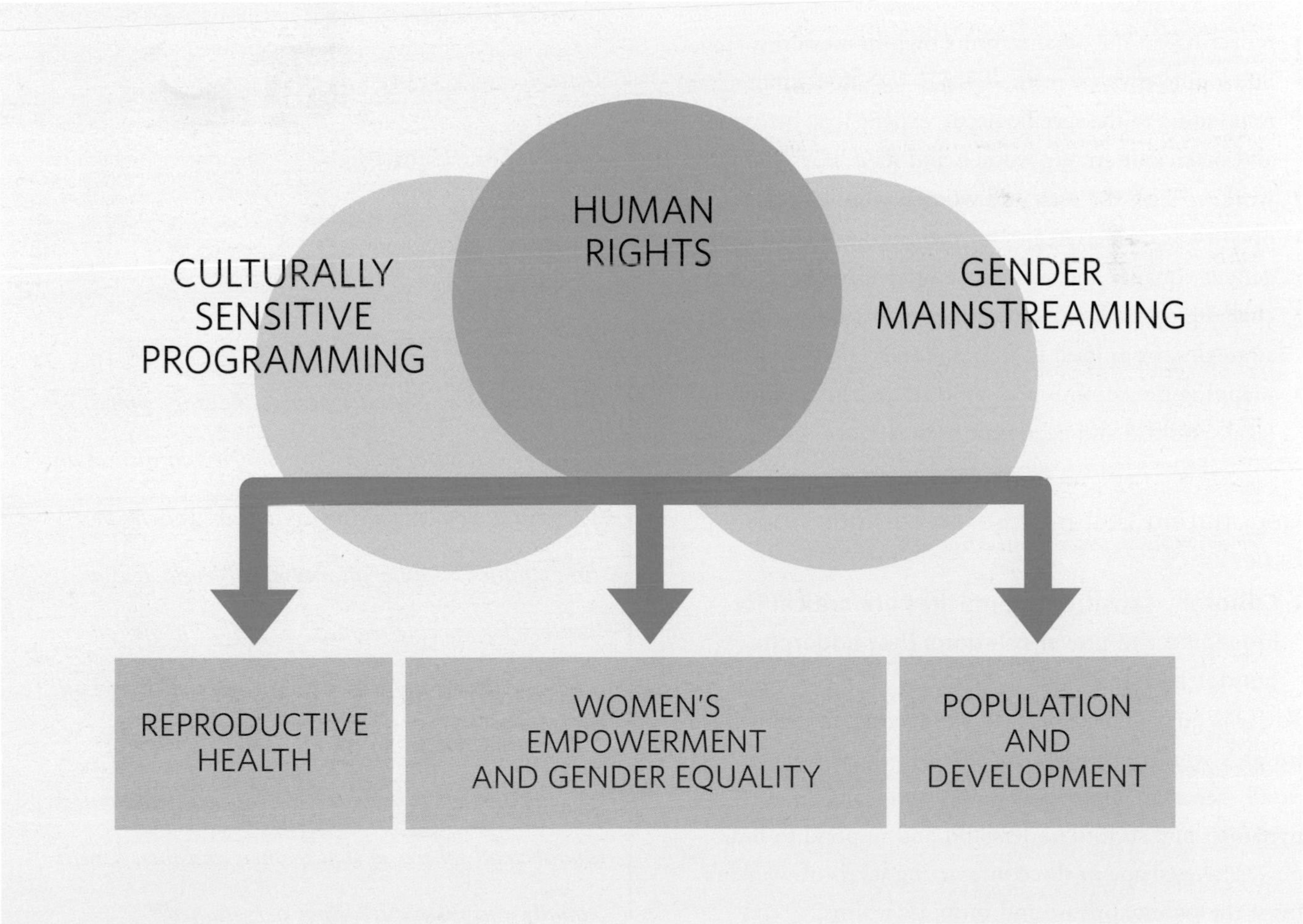

The *24 Tips to Culturally Sensitive Programming* (see box 2 in Chapter 1) identify useful guidelines for engaging with cultures in ways that can facilitate transformative change from within. Transformative change often entails cultural politics.

> Cultural politics is "… the process enacted when sets of actors shaped by, and embodying, different cultural meanings and practices come into conflict with each other…. When movements deploy alternative conceptions of women, nature, race, economy, democracy, or citizenship that unsettle dominant cultural meaning, they enact a cultural politics." [23]

Cultural politics rests on the assumption that systems of meanings are not bound and can be discussed, debated, challenged and even changed. However, the ways in which debates and discussions are introduced is important. Effecting change requires:

- willingness to learn about and understand people's cultural frameworks;
- reflecting on the organization's own frameworks;
- developing effective methodologies for understanding and responding to the specific needs, experiences, perceptions and behaviour among women and men, boys and girls;
- working with the men and women who have developed their own strategies for promoting human rights, gender equality and women's empowerment;
- challenging systems of meanings through a variety of strategies, from local to international levels; and
- mapping the community, national and international legal, political and economic contexts.

Negotiating Cultures: Seven Lessons from Experience

1. Culturally sensitive approaches are critical for loosening the power relations that underpin gender inequalities.

Power is multidimensional. In supporting national efforts towards women's empowerment and gender equality, culturally sensitive approaches go beyond visible power dynamics and seek to understand and respond to how power takes shape in three interacting levels of women's lives: the public, private and intimate realms.

---

9 CAN DEVELOPMENT INITIATIVES BE GENDER NEUTRAL?

Decisions made in planning an initiative shape the type of impact that it will have on culture. For example:

- A community-based rural water supply initiative could include efforts to involve women as well as men in problem identification and management … **or not**, in which case the strategy reinforces the idea that decision-making is a male function and results in decisions that reflect only the priorities and perceptions of men.

- A governance approach concerned with the reform of the civil service could include research and public consultations on the equality implications of provisions on marriage, divorce, property in marriage, inheritance, etc … **or not**, in which case it ignores aspects of the civil law that in many countries institutionalize discrimination against women.

- An infrastructure initiative that restructures a national telephone company's exchanges, equipment and workforce could include consideration of the gender aspects of the employment restructuring and retraining required for the new system … **or not**, in which case it misses the opportunity to contribute to increased equality in the future workforce of an important employer.

Decisions taken in planning are not neutral with respect to gender equality, even where gender issues are not considered.

Source: Schalkwyk, J. 2001. "Questions About Culture, Gender, Equality and Development Cooperation," pp 5-6. Prepared for and produced by the Canadian International Development Agency, Quebec (CIDA), Quebec.

Mainstreaming a gender perspective is the process of assessing the implications for women and men of any planned action, including legislation, policies or programmes, in all areas and at all levels. It is a strategy for making women's as well as men's concerns and experiences an integral dimension of the design, implementation, monitoring and evaluation of policies and programmes in all political, economic and societal spheres so that women and men benefit equally and inequality is not perpetuated. [24]

- The **public realm** of power refers to the visible face of power as it affects women and men in their jobs, employment, public life, legal rights, etc.
- The **private realm** of power refers to relationships and roles in families, among friends, sexual partnerships and marriage.
- The **intimate realm** of power has to do with one's sense of self, personal confidence, psychology and relationship to body and health.

Washing one's hands of the conflict between the powerful and the powerless means to side with the powerful, not to be neutral.

—Paulo Freire, Brazilian educator

For an individual woman, the experience of power and powerlessness will be different based on race, class or age, and may even be contradictory in different realms of her life. For example, a woman politician who appears confident in public may accept a subordinate role in her family; she may even survive abuse in her private relationships while keeping up with the demands of her public duties.[25]

10 SOCIAL STATUS AND GENDER DISCRIMINATION

Five men raped Devi, a Dalit (from the "untouchable" caste) woman and village development worker in India. The police initially refused to record her complaint, but public protest forced an inquiry and the matter came to trial. The lower court held that the delay in filing the complaint and in obtaining medical evidence showed that she was lying. The court considered it unlikely that a higher-caste man would rape a Dalit woman.

All Dalits, male and female, experience discrimination. Women are already reluctant to report violence against them, and the handling of Devi's case will probably add to their reluctance. It may even encourage further violations, as perpetrators realize that they are not likely to face a challenge. Dalit women will thus be even more marginalized — vulnerable to abuse because of their gender and deemed less worthy of protection on grounds of caste.

Source: Banda, F. and C. Chinkin. 2004. "Gender, Minorities and Indigenous Peoples," p. 15. London: Minority Rights Groups International.

2. Culturally sensitive approaches must respond to variations in needs, experiences and cultures, depending on context and within contexts.

Particular groups can suffer more severe forms of discrimination; their experiences of inequality are compounded as "different discriminations intersect and overlap". In a number of conflicts, sexual violence against minority women has become part of the ritual of ethnic cleansing,[26] as in the former Yugoslavia during the 1990s. Throughout the Rwandan genocide in 1994, Tutsi women were targeted, subjected to sexual abuse and then killed. In Gujarat, India, Muslim women have been sexually abused and held up as symbols of the subjugation and humiliation of the community.[27] Women from minority groups, indigenous women, women from different castes, races, cultures and religions can suffer multiple forms of discrimination, which help to cultivate different approaches to gender inequality. Culturally sensitive approaches must be sensitive to these "intersectionalities".

Intersectionality has been explained through the metaphor of a traffic intersection. "Race, gender, class and other forms of discrimination or subordination are the roads that structure the social, economic or political terrain. It is through these thoroughfares that the dynamics of disempowerment travel." These roads are seen as separate and unconnected but in fact they meet, cross over and overlap, forming complex intersections. Women who are marginalized by their sex, race, ethnicity or other factors [here, it is important to include cultures and religion/faith, which are often overlooked] are located at these intersections. The intersections are dangerous places for women who must negotiate the constant traffic through them to avoid injury and to obtain resources for the normal activities of life. Where systems of race, gender and class domination converge … intervention strategies based solely on the experiences of women who do not share the same class or race backgrounds will be of limited help to women who because of race and class face different obstacles.[28]

There is a significant challenge in applying conceptual knowledge within different contexts. People — including some in development — commonly resort to interpreting contexts based on their own experiences, inherited cultural frameworks, objectives and expectations.[29]

3. Without knowledge of and consideration for how people negotiate their own contexts, well-intentioned policy change can incur more costs than benefits.

Culturally sensitive approaches recognize that social constructions of "gender", "freedom" and "equality" will have different meanings in different cultures. These meanings underpin how people relate, what they consider significant and how they attach significance. In some cultures, women's participation in particular aspects of community life and men's participation in others are not regarded as inequality but as differences in responsibilities and roles. There is a tendency to globalize whatever meanings are prevalent, particularly by Western cultures; however, this approach fails to understand the subtleties of different contexts.

One-size-fits-all interventions can provoke unproductive conflicts, such as when they depict all men as aggressors and tyrants and women as passive, ignorant and powerless to change harmful power relations. Such

Ignorance of [the] contextualized notion of common sense ... has been endemic among policymakers in government and in development institutions .... By ignoring this [common sense], policymakers impose a structured and formulaic set of interventions on societies that ill-serve the purpose of improving well-being. Common sense, understood as part of a cultural system ... is a way of providing a knowledge base that shapes how people understand themselves and provides stability to human interactions.[30]

11 **UNDERSTANDING CULTURAL NORMS IN PROMOTING GENDER EQUALITY AND DEVELOPMENT**

I am often asked, usually by expatriate development workers, whether by intervening on women's behalf we are upsetting the gender roles and relations characteristic of the culture. In other words, are we fearful of imposing our own culture on the culture in which we are working, by initiating projects which impact on gender relations? Are we not leaving women more vulnerable than before, by asking them to step out of their culturally ascribed roles and relations?

The assumptions behind these questions need a close examination. Firstly, it is assumed that the culture of communities we work in as development practitioners are a seamless whole, without any cracks; secondly, that unequal gender relations characterize these cultures, and that there are no challenges to inequality from within the cultures. In fact, it is assumed that to be a woman in such cultures is to be passive, subservient and servile. The passive and subservient woman, who is also a victim, thus becomes the stereotype of these cultures.

The fear that we may be imposing our own cultural values by insisting on promoting gender equity in our development work is a real one. However, it is real not because we have concerns about cultural imperialism, but because we allow our own culture-based assumptions about women to colour the way we receive alternative visions of gender equality. We assume that women in developing countries are passive and docile, and that our own view of gender roles, norms and practices is true for everyone. We also fail to recognize the everyday forms of resistance put up by subordinated groups, because these forms of resistance may not correspond to our experience.

Source: Mukhopadhyay, M. 1995. "Gender Relations, Development Practice and 'Culture'." *Gender and Development* 3 (1):13-18. Oxford: Routledge, part of the Taylor & Francis Group.

crude oversimplification can disrupt families and communities and produce a backlash against the interventions, playing into the hands of those who oppose women's empowerment and gender equality. Negotiating cultures requires recognizing and working from the cultural interpretations within different contexts.

4. Culturally sensitive approaches must recognize and learn from local resistance.

Those who hold power and seek to impose meanings in their own interest may oppose gender equality. They describe policies and programmes that aim to promote gender equality as "cultural tampering" or attempts to impose "Western" values as opposed to recognizing people's right to their cultures. The assumptions beneath these arguments are, first, that cultures are fixed and, second, that there is no internal resistance to inequalities. Such assumptions misrepresent women's histories, their opinions and their actions. They also obscure men's roles in challenging patriarchy.

For example, Argentina's Mothers of the Plaza de Mayo recently completed 30 years of activism. The group was formed in 1977 by mothers and female relatives of the *desaparecidos* – those who were arrested without warrants and "disappeared" during the years of the military dictatorship (1976 to 1983). The women organized to demand justice for their children, marching around Plaza de Mayo in Buenos Aires, the seat of government, wearing white scarves symbolizing their children's diapers and their condition as mothers. "The denunciation of torture and murder by plain, hitherto 'apolitical' women had deep impact because the common cultural perception was that selfless mothers would not participate in political movements."[31]

Before their children disappeared, these women were traditional housewives and mothers, tending to the well-being of their families from the safety of their homes. In going out in public to stage their protest and seek justice, the mothers crossed another, invisible threshold, politicizing the private realm and revolutionizing motherhood by extending mothers' duties and concerns into the national and even international arenas.[32] To them, "[t]o be a mother also meant fighting for the rights of their children, left voiceless by the government, and carrying on their children's work and memory in their absence".[33] This involved

---

12   OUR BEST DEFENDERS ARE OURSELVES

Excerpts from an interview with Marie Josee Lokongo Bosiko, Vice President of the National Union of Congolese Workers, shows how people strategically draw from both their cultural norms and formal rights in dealing with real life situations:

What are the main difficulties faced by Congolese women [who want] to become trade unionists? The first obstacle is gaining acceptance from men, who believe that a woman's place is in the home, not a trade union. I got involved in the trade union movement when I was very young. We were afraid of men back then. But we have to work together to ensure that women can take their rightful place in unions. People have to understand that a union with many women members is a strong union, because having women taking part in union activities and recruiting other women is a huge asset. Unequal access to trade union education and training is another problem facing women workers. Most training opportunities are given to men, without the 30 per cent quota for women's partici-pation being respected. Also, married women must have advance permission from their husband to take part in courses outside the country. The Congolese Family Code requires this in its Article 448. The Family Code actual-ly stipulates that a woman must receive her husband's permission to do any-thing of any consequence. We have to teach women how to circumvent these problems. It's important to be well organized, because if you go home after a union meeting and your husband sees that the children have been left unat-tended, he's not going to want you to go to the next meeting. So we ask women to reconcile their roles as a wife, a mother and a worker. As a trade union-ist who worked my way up from the grassroots to the level of vice president, I'm in a position to say that reconciling these roles is possible. We are, of course, fighting for amendment of all the legal dispositions, which are con-trary to the rights of women.

Do your husband and family support your trade union work? Yes. As long as it is accepted that a woman is faithful and does her job well, there is no reason to stop her from being an activist, because her husband, her family and her com-munity all share in the fruit of her work as a unionist....

What about sexual harassment? It's a major problem. We urge women to report any cases of this nature. It was, in fact, the theme of our International Women's Day campaign this year: "No to sexual violence against women". If a man is reported as soon as he starts to harass a woman, he will think twice about it; he'll understand that it isn't right. The perpetrators of harassment should be punished, and once they are, the problem will perhaps diminish. But women can also be harassers. We advise women how to respond when confronted with sexual harassment.

Source: Interview conducted by Samuel Grumiau, 28 August 2007. For the Resisting Women Network, Brussels. www.resistingwomen.net/spip.php?article157, accessed September 2008.

putting themselves at risk and disputing the meaning of their activities with the authorities.

Women testified that participation in the movement was empowering for them. María del Rosario de Cerruti explained: "*One of the things that I simply will not do now is shut up. The women of my generation in Latin America have been taught that the man is always in charge and the woman is silent even in the face of injustice.... Now I know that we have to speak out about the injustices publicly. If not, we are accomplices. I am going to denounce them publicly without fear. This is what I learned.*"

5. Culturally sensitive approaches are necessary for locating actual and potential alliances.

"The equal rights and inherent dignity of all members of the human family are affirmed by the world's religious traditions and enshrined in the Universal Declaration of Human Rights, the Beijing Platform for Action, and the Millennium Development Goals, in which governments and donors renewed their pledge to uphold women's rights and also endorsed women's empowerment as integral to eradicating poverty and to achieving sustainable development."[34] Yet, some aspects of religious discourse and some traditional practices can harm women and men and perpetuate gender inequality and human rights violations. Hence, the importance of seeking alliances with those who can influence behaviour and work together to change these realities. Alliances that span the domains of faith, human rights and gender equality are at the cutting edge of global, regional and local transformations. To realize these critical and cross-dimensional alliances requires an appreciation of the different perspectives, mandates, methods of communication and even pace of each set of actors – e.g., a culturally sensitive approach. For example, the Women, Faith and Development Alliance draws together specific faith-based and inter-faith religious groups, youth, women's rights organizations, corporations and international development organizations in a concerted effort to promote gender equality. What brings these different constituencies together is a shared vision of what constitutes human dignity, but what will enable them to work together will be a pragmatism about the context each comes from and is accountable to. In supporting the Alliance, UNFPA is adapting its culturally

We will be talking about culture and development but we must realize that there is also, among us … a culture of how we do our development work. Who makes the decisions often determines the kinds of decisions that get made. But also HOW the decision-making is structured in any organization also determines the constraints. For instance, if men are always the decision-makers, does that guarantee that women's voices will be heard?[36]

sensitive approach to facilitate constructive dialogue and collaboration among people with a variety of aims and organizational backgrounds.

6. Cultures are contested; differences in values and norms may or may not support gender equality.

Some of these internal contestations come from men, through projects such as Men for Gender Equality Now. This project is part of the African Women's Development and Communication Network (FEMNET). It was initiated by a consultation among men on gender-based violence in Kenya. Since 2001, the men's network has expanded and now works with men across different countries. The project has the following key objectives:

- Promote understanding of gender concepts and practice and promote gender equality.
- Create awareness about and share information and experiences on HIV and AIDS and its relationship to human rights.
- Support survivors of gender-based violence (GBV) by providing emergency referral and follow-up services.
- Network and collaborate with other actors around GBV and HIV and AIDS.
- Conduct research on GBV's prevalence.
- Build the capacity of its members to understand, promote and apply gender equality principles and approaches in their relations and communities.
- Generate the resources required to support activities such as working for government and donor support.[35]

There is now wide agreement that gender equality must involve men.

Culturally sensitive approaches acknowledge that men are a heterogeneous group for whom gender equality has different meanings. At the same time, these approaches advocate and delineate how to involve men in discussions and actions on gender equality to transform gender relations, and around more specific objectives, such as reducing maternal mortality rates and ending gender-based violence.

These specific objectives, which are also central to the MDGs, depend fundamentally on tackling the relationships of power within families, communities and the state that lead to abuse of women's and girls' rights. Tackling adverse relationships necessarily requires working with the men, women, youth, boys and girls who are involved or become involved in these relationships, and working together with those who influence their attitudes and behaviour. Furthermore, some of the most durable changes come when men work with other men and boys to promote gender equality and empower women.

Since 1995, national and international development institutions have shifted from a "women in development" to a "gender and development" (GAD) paradigm. This shift reflects the recognition that gender equality and women's empowerment can only be achieved if men are actively involved in challenging patriarchal structures and, more personally, if their own relationships of power with women are the objects of change." The GAD framework has revealed that men also have different approaches to and experiences of gender equality, and that there are groups of men who are interested in transforming gender relations, not only in women's interests but in their own. The GAD framework has also helped to uncover power relations among men; while men do not suffer the domination that some women encounter, the masculine order can have adverse consequences for men who do not conform to the stereotypes.

In October 2007, academics, policymakers and practitioners who attended the conference "Politicizing Masculinities: Beyond the Personal" confirmed that despite the GAD framework, men and women are still being categorized in unhelpful ways: "The 'men as problems, women as victims' discourse still holds sway.... Both [views] rest on essentialisms that are rarely brought into question. Furthermore, the current work on men and masculinities needs to go beyond how men act in personal domains to broader questions on power relations and core equity issues, such as equal pay and entitlements, representation in politics, and changes to institutions that sustain the gender order. An individual man may be willing but the institutional setting or the peer group culture pushes in the other direction."[20]

▲ Traditions may persist in modern settings – but sometimes reminders are needed.
© Sven Torfinn

Practitioners told of their work in challenging institutions:

Reaching out to raise critical consciousness of men in poor areas (South Africa)
Mbuyiselo Botha: "We have an innovative and creative way of reaching men … we go to the shebeens [local bars]. These places are very important because they are where issues of masculinity are entrenched. We first get buy-in from the shebeen owner … then we ask men if we can talk to them about what it means to be a man. You find various responses. In one incident, a young man said, 'All women are witches.' Then I asked him, 'Do you mean even your mother?

She's one of those witches?' He agreed, but this was captured on national television, and when he arrived home, his mother chucked him away!"

Promoting political consciousness of gender and masculinities (Nicaragua)
Patrick Walsh: "We have developed a community intervention strategy which works with men in the contexts of their communities. Men live in the communities, they live with women, they live in families – they are not just isolated men. As part of that, we run a training course for 20 to 25 men from the community, who, ten times during the year, have a one-day workshop to give them the space to reflect and analyze from their own perspectives and experiences. There is a thematic logic to the workshops, working initially on what it means to be men and women, and the characteristics of masculinity and femininity in Nicaraguan society; then the whole issue of what work we do, what work women do, the value that's given to that; moving into power and violence; then moving into sexuality …. What we end up doing is promoting processes of personal development and growth for men, starting from a gender analysis … enabling men to look at what are called feminine attributes and show that these are human characteristics, human values and human possibilities that we as men can also take on as part of our masculinity."[39]

7. Negotiating cultures for gender equality, women's empowerment and human rights requires reflective, critical and comprehensive approaches.
In conformity with the global consensus at ICPD, UNFPA is committed to attacking, at their roots, some of the most pervasive forms of gender discrimination in public, private and intimate spaces: reproductive health inequities, gender-based violence, economic discrimination and harmful traditional practices. It is important to UNFPA's programming strategy that it collaborates not only with governments but with local organizations and individuals who have been advocating change. For example, in Mauritania, local midwives broke the culture of silence that had long surrounded rape, and which often resulted in the victims of rape being imprisoned and the

perpetrators freed. UNFPA supported the collection of statistics on sexual violence and the establishment of a centre to meet the needs of survivors. UNFPA helped to move these issues from private to public spaces, building consensus among local imams, judges, police, government officials and members of the public that women must be protected from sexual violence. These interventions have led to a notable reduction in the incidence of rape and observed changes in attitudes to rape, as well as to the collection of quality data on rape.[40]

In Ethiopia, UNFPA supports the *Berhane Hewan* project, which provides adolescent girls with education to help them delay marriage. Though Ethiopian law prohibits marriage before the age of 18, early marriage is a longstanding cultural practice that often results in reproductive health problems such as obstetric fistula or in maternal death. Educational opportunities are important because they offer girls a different perception of themselves and their potential. They also lead to changes in community perceptions, as families are involved in the planning and implementation of the education project.[41]

Cultural politics are controversial, and consensus can be difficult to achieve. In supporting women's empowerment in countries as diverse as Nicaragua, Chad, Viet Nam and the Lao People's Democratic Republic, UNFPA has been working with various cultural actors. From faith-based organizations (such as the Group of Islamic Associations for Questions of Population and Development in Niger) to traditional associations (e.g., the Association of African Traditional Leaders) to indigenous peoples networks (e.g., the *Enlace Continental de Mujeres Indigenas de las Américas*, Region Sur, coordinated by another indigenous organization – Chirapaq – in Peru), UNFPA uses the culture lens to ensure local acceptance and engagement on issues including gender equality and reproductive health. These types of interventions are producing durable changes.

4 Negotiating Culture: Reproductive Health and Reproductive Rights

Reproductive rights ... derive from the recognition of the basic right of all individuals and couples to make decisions about reproduction free from discrimination, coercion or violence. They include the right to the highest standard of health and the right to determine the number, timing and spacing of children. They comprise the right to safe child-bearing, and the right of all individuals to protect themselves from HIV and other sexually transmitted infections.[1]

Culturally sensitive approaches seek to understand the diverse meanings people give to rights, reproduction and health, and the different ways in which social groups make claims on the reproductive body, sex and childbearing. There is a wide range of discussion and dispute on these issues. It is a mistake to assume that all people within a culture have the same rationale for action, or that apparently similar cultural norms and practices have the same meanings.

Culturally sensitive approaches must be open to the unexpected. Both men and women take part in shaping the gender order and social expectations concerning the male and female body, and in varied and unpredictable ways. For

To understand what is happening in other cultures requires recognition of the weight and influence of one's own framework, as well as acknowledgement that people may use entirely different lenses to interpret the same circumstances. Understanding the languages of different cultures does not mean accepting the meanings ascribed; but it can provide a useful platform for dialogue and action.[2]

example, some men become advocates for change in favour of women: Men for Gender Equality Now in Kenya is a "network of men working to end gender-based violence and the spread of HIV and AIDS through prevention, service provision to the victims and awareness-creation focusing on the role of men as agents of change".[3]

◄ *Everyone has a right to information and services to protect their health. What these young people in Belize are learning about HIV and AIDS could save their lives.*
© Carina Wint

Conversely, women may share male views of practices that harm them: "Violence against women in Gaza basically means domestic violence," says research consultant Aitemad Muhanna. "Women are beaten by their husbands, beaten by their fathers, and even beaten by their brothers…. Most of this violence is hidden. It's not recorded and not discussed." Most women do not believe they are victims of violence, even though their husband may abuse them, because they consider it "a husband's right" – an attitude men share.[4]

Understanding the diversities of cultural meanings is essential for designing and implementing effective cooperation for change within a cultural context. For example, all societies value children, and childlessness is often stigmatized to a greater or lesser extent. Stigma affects the identity of women as mothers rather than men as fathers, especially where childbearing and motherhood gives women their primary identity and access to economic resources. Cultural understandings about what men and women contribute to procreation may also stigmatize women. In parts of Egypt and India, people believe that men contribute a fully formed foetus; the quality of the woman's womb and menstrual blood determines how the foetus develops.[5] Some Asian and African cultures define infertility as women's inability to produce sons. Some societies consider infertile

women to have been cursed. Almost all see "barren" women in a negative way. Such notions reinforce patriarchy and perpetuate a valuation of women based on fertility. Women themselves may assess their own and other women's worth on their ability to reproduce.

Contraception is widely used in developing countries to promote reproductive health, but women who fear infertility are unlikely to adopt it. Qualitative and demographic studies of contraceptive behaviour in India show that women are most likely to accept contraceptive methods (especially irreversible ones such as sterilization) **after** they have achieved their desired number of children, rather than seek it as a means of spacing pregnancies.[6] Women believe that contraceptive devices preserve their reproductive potential, which is "spent" by childbearing.[7] Cultural knowledge of this sort is important for determining how to intervene in these contexts.

Female Genital Mutilation/Cutting: The Value of Cultural Knowledge

Cultural knowledge is invaluable for helping men and women make practical choices, for example, about contraception. It also provides strategic guidance in especially difficult situations. With the benefit of cultural knowledge, UNFPA has been working with partners to tackle harmful practices such as female genital mutilation/cutting (FGM/C).

The Programme of Action of the 1994 International Conference on Population and Development (ICPD) ranks female genital mutilation/cutting among the "harmful practices meant to control women's sexuality" and describes it as "a violation of basic rights and a major lifelong risk to women's health" (para. 7.35). The consensus is that "governments and communities should urgently take steps to stop the practice" (para. 7.40).

Historical and cultural studies reveal the cultural significance of FGM/C. For example, some African societies consider female "circumcision" to be critical for group membership; it is a woman's initiation into adulthood. Some societies regard "uncircumcised" women as abnormal. The clitoris and labia are viewed as male organs, and a woman becomes feminine only when these organs are removed.[8] The practice is also considered important for hygiene, cleanliness and beauty. In some cultures, there is

---

15 THE SOCIAL STIGMA OF INFERTILITY

The medical definition of primary infertility is inability to produce offspring after a year of cohabitation. After the birth of a child, reproductive tract infections may result in secondary infertility. Although infertility can affect both women and men, women experience most of the fears and social costs of secondary infertility. Infertility remains an unrecognized reproductive rights issue. Despite high prevalence in many poor regions of the world, particularly in sub-Saharan Africa,* infertility is not considered a matter for public health policy. Planners concerned with reducing high fertility ignore infertility, though the two are connected.** Infertility carries a high social cost for individuals, especially women, and couples who are unable to bear children.

*Source: Feldman-Savelsburg, P. 2002. "Is Infertility an Unrecognised Public Health Problem: The View from the Cameroon Grassfields," *Infertility Around the Globe: New Thinking on Childlessness, Gender, and Reproductive Technologies*, edited by M. Inhron and F. Van Balen. Berkeley: University of California Press.
**Source: Inhorn, M. and Van Balen, F. 2002. *Infertility Around the Globe: New Thinking on Childlessness, Gender, and Reproductive Technologies*. Berkeley: University of California Press.

---

16 FGM/C IN CULTURAL CONTEXT

The local appellation for female "circumcision" in many of the African societies where it is practised is synonymous with the term cleanliness or purification (for example, *tahara* in Egypt, *tahur* in Sudan and *sili-ji* among the Bambarra in Mali). In such societies, women who have not been "circumcised" are considered unclean. Such women, in the rare instances in which they exist, are not allowed to handle food and water. "Uncircumcised" female genitals in societies that practice female "circumcision" are further viewed as oversized and ugly... Members of such societies generally believe that if not excised, a woman's genitals are likely to grow so long as to hang down between her legs, thus becoming unsightly.

Source: Njoh, A. 2006. *Tradition, Culture and Development in Africa*, p. 97. Hampshire: Burlington. Ashgate Publishing Company.

Cultural insights illuminate how context influences individual reproductive choices. In turn, this structures the kinds of interventions needed to accommodate mindsets and behavioural patterns. This is part of the value of culturally sensitive approaches.

a belief that without it, babies can be damaged during childbirth as would a man's penis during intercourse. Some believe that the practice can promote fertility.

Understanding these multiple meanings is important, not for validating the practice but for acknowledging its roots and providing a basis for dialogue and action. UNFPA has found that this cultural knowledge has been essential to its cooperative strategy of finding culturally acceptable alternatives.

In Guinea-Bissau, for example, recent (2006) indicators show that FGM/C is still widely practised: 44.5 per cent of girls and women aged 15 to 49 years are affected. Following a number of failed initiatives to end FGM/C, the United Nations Children's Fund (UNICEF) and UNFPA partnered with Tostan, a non-governmental organization (NGO) with a good track record in Senegal, Guinea, Gambia, Burkina Faso and Mauritania. Tostan's approach is to engage the community in respectful discussions on human rights. People are also encouraged to talk about concerns within the area and to review problem-solving approaches. This process of engagement often culminates with a collective decision to abandon FGM/C. Community acceptance avoids social pressures on individual families and girls.[9]

17 HELPING GIRLS ESCAPE FEMALE GENITAL MUTILATION/CUTTING AND CHILD MARRIAGE IN KENYA

Certain groups in Kenya, such as the Somali, Kisii and Masai, practise female genital cutting as a routine process which prepares young girls for marriage (Kenyan Demographic and Health Survey 2003). Usually carried out before a girl reaches 14 years of age, female "circumcision" is seen as enabling girls to become "clean" before they enter adulthood. In its severe form every part of the genitalia is removed, without anaesthesia. The physical health risks include trauma and bleeding, and in later life difficult childbearing and heightened risk of sexually transmitted infections including HIV. Psychological damage is incalculable.

In partnership with UNFPA, the community-based project *Tasaru Ntomonok* Initiative (TNI) has been successful in replacing the cultural value represented by FGM/C, at the same time recognizing its importance as a rite of passage. One of the strengths of its approach has been to offer alternatives to FGM/C, in a culturally appropriate way, as part of girls' transition to adulthood. Older women continue to act as godmothers to girls when they come of age. The girls also undergo the customary period of seclusion where they are made aware of sex and reproduction, and now learn about the importance of reproductive and sexual health. Alternative ceremonies now take place at the time when FGM/C was traditionally performed, and the women who used to do the cutting have other sources of income. Men's involvement is vital. Fathers need to be reassured that their daughters will be marriageable and a potential source of income, and young men need to understand that they will have suitable wives.

If for any reason the community does not accept the alternative rite to FGM/C, TNI offers shelter to girls who request it. The project has been helped nationally by the Children's Act of 2001, which prohibits FGM/C and early marriage, with penalties of imprisonment of up to 12 months and a fine up to $735.

Source: UNFPA. 2007. "Kenya: Creating a Safe Haven, and a Better Future, for Maasai Girls Escaping Violence." Chapter 6 in *Programming to Address Violence Against Women: Ten Case Studies*. New York. UNFPA.

Probing Cultures

"If cultures are, in part, conversations and contestations – including about questions such as reproductive health and rights … some voices … are more privileged than others."[10] People largely accept cultural norms and conform to expected behaviours.

Some of the most dramatic changes occur when the guardians of cultural norms and practices advocate for them. In Cambodia, Buddhist nuns and monks are prominent in the struggle to combat HIV.[11] In Zimbabwe, local indigenous leaders are in the forefront. Some of these very leaders had earlier encouraged practices such as polygamy, child marriage and a ban on contraceptives. Now, as one leader acknowledged, "We have to preach the anti-AIDS gospel if we want to remain relevant to

If culture is a factor in transmission and impact [of HIV], it follows that prevention and care require a cultural approach.[13]

our members." The leaders' new doctrine has weight within the communities and is prompting changes in attitudes and practices.[12]

It is important to build alliances with prominent and influential leaders committed to human rights, gender equality or objectives such as HIV prevention. But leaders can also use alliances to entrench their power and authority; while working towards one goal they may block change in other areas. Alliances should therefore seek

---

18 CONTESTING CULTURES WITHIN FAITH COMMUNITIES

One by one, Annie Kaseketi Mwaba buried her husband and four of her children. Then, in 2003, Annie herself fell ill. After several months, she asked her doctor to test her for HIV. Initially, he said no. Most Zambians, after all, regard AIDS as a consequence of immoral behaviour – and Annie was a Christian preacher. Finally, though, he relented, and Annie started her long journey back to life. "I thought HIV was for people who were not going to church," says Annie. "I think I was in deep denial. I didn't want to face this HIV thing. Until one evening, I was reading the Bible. It's like somebody shed light there. If they find you're HIV positive, your life is not in the virus, your life is in Christ."

The following year, Annie's remaining son, then nine years old, underwent treatment for tuberculosis. She decided to have him tested for HIV, and he was positive, too. In fact, his immune system was more compromised than hers had ever been. Now, mother and son are on the mend, and Annie has become a powerhouse in the effort to combat AIDS in Zambia. In a country where any

mention of AIDS used to be taboo, Annie has spoken out, making her painful story the pivot of her effort to change hearts and minds. An elegant woman of 43, she has taken on religious leaders who preached that AIDS stemmed from evil behaviour, that it was okay to let its victims die. "It's amazing how God can use my mess and make it a message," she declares.

Annie talks about attending a workshop for religious leaders, where she spoke about her friend "Grace," a minister who had tested positive after losing her husband and children to AIDS. The response was harsh and unyielding. "She killed her children! She was a prostitute! Let her die!" one leader bellowed. If he were the government, this man continued, he would poison antiretroviral drugs so that AIDS patients would perish. "Then I said that was my story," Annie says softly. "I walked to him and said, 'Do I have to die?' He said, 'No, you don't.'"

She has also reached out in the pews. Not long after Annie discovered she was living with HIV, a woman from her church confided to her that she was

HIV-positive. "I thought about my husband – he might have been positive, and he died because we were silent. How many pastors have we buried?" Annie says. "I thought, 'HIV is very much in the church, in the pews, and we have to break the silence.' I decided the next Sunday, I will divulge my status from the pulpit." She did so, and the floodgates opened. Annie was deluged with congregants who told her that they, too, were living with HIV. "I felt that my coming out gave permission to others to share," she says. Now, Annie works full-time to mobilize Christian and Islamic faith communities to respond to AIDS, and to prevent HIV infection among children. She facilitates community-led initiatives to combat the disease, and identify and help vulnerable households and children, many of them orphans. The faith community, Annie says, now views HIV and AIDS as "not about them – but about us."

Source: The Centre for Development and Population Activities (CEDPA). 2007. "Changing Hearts and Minds From the Pulpit in Zambia: Annie Kaseketi Mwaba." Washington, D.C.: CEDPA. http://www.cedpa.org/content/news/detail/1713, accessed June 2008.

broader objectives such as human rights and gender equality. These larger principles are critical in setting standards for cultural engagement.

Standards should also ensure spaces for dialogue with community members, so that efforts to push for change are not overlooked. In China, UNFPA supports transport workers by providing HIV and AIDS education to migrant travellers. In Belize, UNFPA works with local community organizations, such as 4H, the Cornerstone Foundation, the Cadet Corps, the United Belize Advocacy Movement and the Young Women's Christian Organization to reach community members, particularly children in school, with important messages about HIV prevention. UNFPA supports the everyday activities of barbers in Belize, who speak to customers about HIV.[14]

Comprehensive, culturally sensitive approaches are necessary for HIV prevention. Healthlink Worldwide, a health and development NGO working with vulnerable communities in developing countries, has outlined four reasons why culturally sensitive approaches must be part of a global HIV and AIDS strategy:

- Cultural approaches to HIV and AIDS have built trust and engagement at the community level, increasing the likelihood of prevention.
- Cultural approaches to HIV and AIDS are gaining currency because they interact with the values, beliefs, traditions and social structures – the "webs of significance" – in which people live.
- Where a cultural approach is used in HIV and AIDS communication, there is evidence of wider impact on awareness and attitudes, of stigma reduction, and of more inclusion of people living with HIV and AIDS.
- Culture can offer a real benefit to global strategy for HIV and AIDS if it is re-cast as an opportunity for action and engagement with communities, rather than as a barrier to prevention and bio-medical approaches.

Honour is to live as it is ordered by our religion. The borders of honour should not be passed. I mean, honour is to keep oneself away from the places forbidden by God, not to try to cross the borders. For example, not only his wife, but also his mother, his sister and his neighbour are a man's honour. A man should be careful to protect the honour of others, as he is protecting his own.

—Adana, male, age 30, *imam*[15]

Religion has a privileged place in a wide range of cultures, and people willingly accept – or at least observe – systems of religious belief. Religion is central to many people's lives and influences the most intimate decisions and actions.

Religious meanings of reproduction and reproductive health differ, even within religions, depending on who provides the interpretations. For instance, some cultures interpret the Biblical encouragement to be fruitful and multiply to mean that women should bear as many children as their bodies will allow. In others, the injunction does not prevent individuals or couples from choosing the number and spacing of their children. It is difficult to work with cultures without understanding their debates over religion.

Because people often regard religion as authoritative, a spurious appeal to religion can be used to justify harmful practices, even crimes. In some societies, "honour" crimes and crimes of passion are regarded as sanctioned by religious precepts.

The United Nation's Secretary-General's report, *In-depth Study on all Forms of Violence Against Women*,[16] notes that crimes against women committed in the name of "honour" may occur within the family or within the community. In some Kurdish communities, for example: "Honour crimes take many forms including 'honour killings', forced marriage, coerced marriage to an alleged rapist, unlawful confinement and strict restrictions on women's movement."[17]

People in societies where these practices are common may disagree among themselves about what "honour" implies, but the view of some – the most powerful actors because they are prepared to use violence to bolster their arguments – is that male honour depends on controlling women, particularly in regard to their sexuality. A woman can be dishonoured in a range of situations, such as conducting an extramarital relationship, initiating separation or divorce, an unmarried girl's entering a relationship

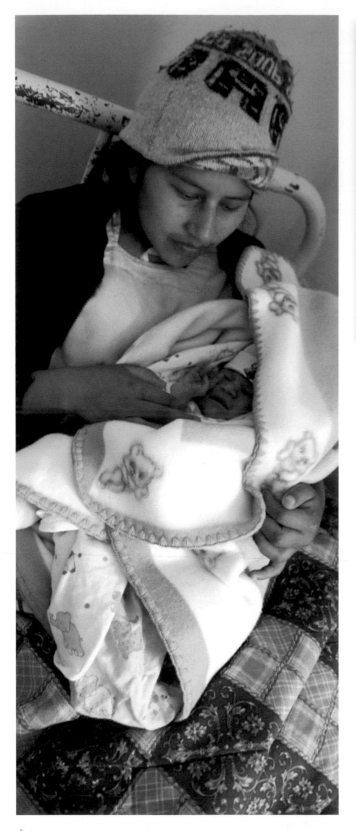

Mother and baby in a hospital in El Alto, Bolivia. Many women prefer to give birth at home – but they need skilled care and referral to a hospital in case of need.
© Tim Weller

19 **THE SOCIAL AND PERSONAL COSTS OF OBSTETRIC FISTULA**

The majority of family members confirmed that women with fistula experienced isolation, mainly as a result of shame, but also due to the fear of harassment or ridicule, or physical weakness that compromised a woman's ability to walk. A minority of family members explicitly mentioned the sadness of living with fistula. For example, one set of parents reported that their daughter experienced sadness and loneliness, and another set of parents said that their daughter was always unhappy because she could not walk properly and could not visit relatives or friends because of shame.

Source: Women's Dignity Project and EngenderHealth. 2006. "Living With Obstetric Fistula: The Devastating Impacts of the Condition and Ways of Coping." New York: EngenderHealth. http://www.engenderhealth.org/files/pubs/maternal-health/Obstetric_Fistula_Brief_3_Impacts_and_Coping.pdf, accessed June 2008.

without permission, or being the victim of rape or kidnapping. All these actions can incur violent retribution on a woman by men in her family, often with the support of women relatives.

In accordance with the articles of CEDAW and the global consensus of ICPD, the United Nations regards "honour" killings as a clear violation of human rights, with no cultural justification. The United Nations General Assembly adopted resolution 55/66 entitled, "Working Towards the Elimination of Crimes Against Women Committed in the Name of Honour", on 4 December 2000. In this resolution, concern was expressed about the continuing occurrence, in all regions of the world, of violence against women, "including crimes against women committed in the name of honour, which take many different forms", and also expressed its concern that "some perpetrators assume that they have some justification for committing such crimes".

The implicit reference here is cultural justifications. The resolution acknowledged the importance of culture and cultural actors very specifically, by calling upon all States "to intensify efforts to prevent and eliminate crimes against women committed in the name of honour, which take many different forms, by using legislative, educational, social and other measures, including the dissemination of information, and *to involve, among others, public opinion leaders, educators, religious leaders, chiefs, traditional leaders and the media* [emphasis added] *in awareness-raising campaigns".* The italicized clause lists the actors which UNFPA, in particular, refers to as "cultural agents of change".

General Assembly resolution 55/68 adopted on 4 December 2000 puts crimes of "honour" in a broader context:

Reaffirming further the call for the elimination of violence against women and girls, especially all forms of commercial sexual exploitation as well as economic exploitation, including trafficking in women and children, female infanticide, crimes committed in the name of honour, crimes committed in the name of passion, racially motivated crimes, the abduction and sale of children, dowry-related violence and deaths, acid attacks and harmful traditional or customary practices, such as female genital mutilation and early and forced marriages....

Many of UNFPA's interventions at the country level are designed to mobilize and support community-based efforts to correct any assertions that religion, or culture more broadly, legitimizes such practices.

Culturally sensitive approaches are important for reaching other critical targets such as MDG 5, which aims for a 75 per cent reduction in maternal deaths between 1990 and 2015. Despite long efforts to reduce maternal mortality in developing countries, numbers have remained essentially unchanged at about 536,000 a year. Ninety-nine per cent of maternal deaths occur in developing countries, the majority in sub-Saharan Africa and South Asia. Cost-effective health interventions could prevent many maternal deaths, but most poor women cannot take advantage of them. There are doubts that MDG 5 will be achieved: Globally, the maternal mortality ratio decreased at less than 1 per cent between 1990 and 2005, compared with the 5.5 per cent needed to achieve MDG 5. Only a few countries have achieved a significant reduction in maternal mortality rates since 1990: China, Cuba, Egypt, Jamaica, Malaysia, Sri Lanka, Thailand and Tunisia.

Many women in the poorest countries survive pregnancy and childbirth but with serious consequences,

20 SAFE MOTHERHOOD AND THE STATUS OF WOMEN IN SOCIETY

- In societies where men traditionally control household finances, women's health expenses are often not a priority.
- Women are often not in a position to decide if, when and with whom to become pregnant or to determine the number, spacing and timing of their children.
- In countries with similar levels of economic development, maternal mortality is inversely proportional to women's status.
- The poorer the household, the greater the risk of maternal death and morbidity.
- Early marriages, female genital mutilation/cutting, too many childbirths and violence signal the violation of a woman's right to make decisions about her own body.

Source: UNFPA. n.d. "Facts About Safe Motherhood." New York: UNFPA. http//www.unfpa.org/mothers/facts.htm. Accessed March 2008.

among them obstetric fistula, anaemia, infertility, damaged pelvic structure, chronic infection, depression and impaired productivity.[18]

Millions of women still do not have control over spacing or limiting pregnancies, nor access to effective contraception. This is the result of ineffective health systems, but there are also social and cultural factors involved. In many cultures, patriarchal frameworks determine notions of masculinity and femininity, as well as the meanings of sexuality, reproduction and rights. The result is that women's needs and rights are paid little attention. It is important to situate women's health within their social and cultural contexts, and to develop culturally sensitive responses.

UNFPA has a long tradition of supporting maternal health facilities and providing crucial supplies such as contraceptives and equipment for emergency obstetric care.

The World Health Organization (WHO) estimates that approximately 2 million women and girls are affected by fistula and a further 50,000 to 100,000 are newly affected annually.[19]

The Fund works nationally, internationally and with communities to improve maternal health. For example, in Nigeria, local leaders are convincing the men in their communities of the value of family planning and of caring for the reproductive health needs of their families and communities. The Ministry of Health, with support from UNFPA, trains the leaders who then spread the messages. "Before the training, it was difficult to convince men of the importance of contraceptives," says Abdulai Abukayode, the *baale* (traditional leader) of Ajengule in Ogun State. "Once they knew more, that changed.... People now want less children, so they can take care of them." Contraceptive prevalence has increased dramatically in Ogun.[20]

Similarly, UNFPA is working with partners to prevent and treat obstetric fistula, and to reintegrate affected girls and women into society. Fistula is especially prevalent in poor, remote regions and among very young women whose bodies are not fully capable of childbirth. It results from extensive tissue damage during periods of prolonged and obstructed labour, which leaves a tear between the vagina and bladder or the vagina and rectum. The baby frequently dies, and the mother is left incontinent. Fistula is the cause of great shame: Husbands, families and communities may shun affected women and force them to live in isolation. Yet, obstetric fistula is preventable; it is not common in wealthier areas, where women have good access to quality maternal health care.

In the absence of close engagement with the communities concerned, obstetric fistula has been overlooked and its victims neglected. An effective response calls for culturally sensitive approaches, not only to communicate with girls and women about prevention and treatment, but also to reduce stigma and raise fistula as a policy concern. UNFPA is supporting efforts to prevent fistula and treat and rehabilitate affected girls and women. For example, in Sudan, UNFPA is supporting the Saudi Hospital, El Fasher, where girls and women benefit from reconstructive surgery.[21] In Eritrea, UNFPA partnered with surgeons from Stanford University to strengthen national capacity to treat fistula.[22] In the Democratic Republic of the Congo, UNFPA has worked with the Ministry of Health to stage a national campaign, which included treatment.[23]

Culture, Masculinity and Sexual and Reproductive Health

Work on reproductive health and rights calls for culturally sensitive approaches because the issues go to the heart of culture. It also requires a focus on gender relations and men. Following the United Nations World Conference on Women in Mexico City in 1975 and the United Nations Decade for Women 1976 to 1985, the Programme of Action of the 1994 Cairo International Conference on Population and Development (ICPD) challenged men to play their full part in the fight for gender equality within the framework of reproductive health and population and development. The Platform for Action of the 1995 Fourth World Conference on Women in Beijing restated the principle of shared responsibility, and argued that women's concerns could be addressed only in partnership with men.[24] It called on men to support women by sharing childcare and household work equally, and also called for male responsibility in HIV and sexually transmitted infection (STI) prevention.

The 26th special session of the General Assembly in 2001 recognized the need to challenge gender attitudes and gender inequalities in relation to HIV and AIDS through the active involvement of men and boys. Its "Declaration of Commitment on HIV/AIDS" addressed men's roles and responsibilities related to reducing the spread and impact of HIV and AIDS, especially the need to engage men in challenging the gender inequalities driving the epidemic.[25] A decade after Cairo, the 48th session of the United Nations Commission on the Status of Women in 2004 called on governments, entities of the United Nations system and other stakeholders to, *inter alia,* encourage the active involvement of men and boys in eliminating gender stereotypes, encourage men to participate in preventing and treating HIV and AIDS, implement programmes to enable men to adopt safe and responsible sexual practices, support men and boys to prevent gender-based violence, and implement programmes in schools to accelerate gender equality.

Male power – patriarchy – continues in many cultures. Some analysts[26] acknowledge that the "... ongoing challenge to the reproductive health framework is how to characterize men's possible influences and to assess their

▲ *The next best thing to avoiding obstetric fistula is surgery to repair it. Rupbahar is one of the "lucky" ones, seen with her mother in a fistula camp in Bangladesh.*
© UNFPA

impact on women's and children's health." However, men are also subject to culture, which calls for closer attention both to men's experiences of gender and its inequalities and their responsibility for it.

The evidence suggests that cultural pressures around gender increase men's vulnerability to sexual ill-health. Social constructions of masculinity and sexuality can increase risk-taking and reduce the likelihood of men seeking help. According to national surveys of men aged 15 to 54 over the past 10 years in 39 countries, men's sexual initiation tends to be earlier than women's, and men have more sexual partners, both outside and within marriage.[27] In almost all of the countries surveyed, most men 20 to 24 years old report sexual initiation before their 20th birthday. Although this varies significantly by region, in some countries up to 35 per cent report sexual initiation before their 15th birthday. These data, however, do not include all groups in all regions, leaving out industrial countries and key groups such as unmarried men, men in prison, the military, migrants or refugees, many of whom are sexually active. Many cultures see variety in sexual partners as essential to men's nature, so that men will inevitably seek multiple partners for sexual release.[28] Global sexual behaviour studies indicate that heterosexual men, both married and single, as well as homosexual and bisexual men, have higher reported rates of partner change than women.[29]

There has been increasing interest in understanding this behaviour in gendered terms. Seeking common themes, some research suggests that traditional notions of masculinity are strongly associated with a wide range of risk-taking behaviour, and that "… cultural and societal expectations and norms create an environment where risk is acceptable and even encouraged for 'real' men".[30] A qualitative research project in nine Latin American countries found that young men aged 10 to 24 years were far more concerned with achieving and preserving their masculinity than their health.[31]

Cultural pressures around masculinity that fuel men's need to prove sexual potency can encourage seeking multiple partners and exercising authority over women. This

INVOLVING MEN IN PROMOTING GENDER EQUALITY

"Program H" promotes gender-equitable norms and behaviours among young men in low-income settings, helping them to reflect upon and question traditional norms of "manhood". The programme, developed by *Instituto Promundo* based in Rio de Janeiro, Brazil and three other NGOs in Brazil and Mexico, identified two factors: gender-equitable male role models and peer groups; and reflecting on the consequences of violence.

Programme staff developed a manual of activities on gender, sexual health, violence and relationships. The manual addressed sexism and homophobia, which is also directed at non-macho men and independent women. At the same time, a social marketing campaign portrayed gender-equitable behaviour as cool and hip, using radio, billboards, postcards and dances. In Brazil, the intervention showed significant shifts in gender norms at six months and 12 months. Young men with more equitable norms were between four and eight times less likely to report STI symptoms, with additional improvements at 12 months after the intervention.

Program H (the "H" refers to homens, or "men" in Portuguese) relies on research to understand the variations of gender attitudes and practices among its target audience, and communicates through media drawn from and appealing to youth culture.

Source: Pulerwitz, J.; G. Barker, and M. Segundo. 2004. "Promoting Healthy Relationships and HIV/STI Prevention for Young Men: Positive Findings from an Intervention Study in Brazil". Washington, D.C.: Population Council/Horizons Communications Unit.

---

times of need.[33] Data from South Africa indicate that men are much less likely than women to use voluntary counselling and testing (VCT) services. Men account for only 21 per cent of all clients receiving VCT[34] and only 30 per cent of those in treatment.[35] Men access antiretroviral therapy (ART) later than women in the disease's progression, with more compromised immune systems and at greater cost to the public health system.[36] These discrepancies appear to reflect men's belief that seeking health services is a sign of weakness, rather than higher infection rates among women.[37]

Cultural pressures around masculinity can also give rise to feelings of anxiety among men about their sexuality. Men are more likely to mention concerns about sexual performance than STIs or HIV. This may be especially true for young men, who are discouraged by families, teachers and others from talking about their bodies and issues such as pubertal changes.[38] Boys may know more about women's bodies than about their own. Boyhood ignorance can translate into lifelong difficulties in talking about sex and finding out facts.

Cultural pressures and expectations, ignorance and anxiety encourage risk-taking, and expose not only boys and men but also their sex partners to sexual and reproductive ill-health. However, many men do not consider their behaviours to be risky; they may understand their sexuality as a natural drive and sex as a biological necessity, which obviates the sense of risk.

It is also important to put notions of risk in their social and economic contexts. For example, the city of São Paulo has the highest prevalence of HIV infection in Brazil, but young men from low-income communities are probably less afraid of AIDS than of accidents, violence or drugs.

Culturally sensitive approaches must acknowledge the contexts within which boys and men operate. Conventional explanations suggest that young men get their ideas of sexual entitlement from unequal gender relations that privilege men over women; male power makes gender violence normal. Culturally sensitive approaches go beyond this explanation to investigate the relationship between social and political contexts and resulting cultural norms, and the conditions under which men and women resist them. For example, it

---

can lead, for example, to men forcing sex on unwilling partners as a result of a perceived need to prove themselves.[32] As one young man noted, "Unless a woman cries while having sex, your masculinity is not proven." Pressures around masculinity, coupled with sexual repression, result in increasing rates of rape and other forms of violence against women. The results can damage not only women's health but their social acceptance. The raped woman may even be encouraged to marry her rapist to avoid the scandal of being "deflowered". Married women who bring charges of rape have sometimes found themselves imprisoned for adultery.

Many cultures associate masculinity with a sense of invulnerability, and socialize men to be self-reliant, not to show their emotions and not to seek assistance in

is possible to link young men's sexual violence in apartheid South Africa with the system's political coercion. Similarly, work on gender norms with low-income young men in Rio de Janeiro should acknowledge the violence and trauma that many of them experience as they grow up, which is related to racism, economic inequality and state violence. Brazil has one of the highest rates of homicide in the world, and rates of homicide for men are over 12 times higher than for women. Men of African descent have a 73 per cent higher rate of homicide than men of European descent. Culturally sensitive approaches avoid the tendency to separate the cultural from the political, and consider instead how they interact. This enables a much more effective response to men's differing needs in differing contexts.

Culturally sensitive approaches recognize that generalizations about boys, girls, men and women, groups and communities, mask important diversities. Culturally sensitive approaches are interested in these diversities, and the diverse solutions that individuals and communities evolve. Culturally sensitive approaches to issues such as infertility, fertility and maternal health appreciate why people make the choices they do within their social and cultural contexts; what responses are already on the ground; what sorts of alliances are available; what sorts of interventions are appropriate; how to communicate for maximum impact; and how to allow that knowledge to inform programming, rather than impose pre-defined solutions.

5 Negotiating Culture: Poverty, Inequality and Population

Sustainable development decreases poverty and inequality and promotes socio-economic inclusion for all groups. Unequal distribution of the products of economic growth increases both the extent and the depth of poverty. Poverty and inequality limit access to resources and opportunities. In this reality, cultural components such as family relationships, patterns of human activity, coping strategies and prescribed and unsanctioned behaviours are important and consistent features. Poor health and low levels of education make it more difficult to translate additional income into improved well-being, preventing people from establishing or reaching personal goals.[1]

Some 750 million people face socio-economic discrimination or disadvantage because of their cultural identities.[2] Policies may deliberately exclude them or, by limiting access to services and funding, may expose them to a life of poverty. Minorities subject to discrimination and disadvantage are more likely to be poor. The poor are less healthy than the better-off, use health services less, are less likely to avoid unhealthy practices or adopt healthy ones and are disadvantaged in other areas that determine health status.[3] Life expectancies are short and maternal mortality and morbidity are high. Poor women in particular are bound by aspects of tradition and culture detrimental to their well-being.

Recent analyses emphasize that relationships of inequality sustain the structures and processes that keep people in poverty. Economic and political analysis must be placed within cultural contexts, examining not only the types of choices made but the local conditions and external dynamics within which they are made. This is a requirement to substantiate and improve the resulting policy advice.

◀ *A family business in Kathmandu, Nepal. In many cultures, doing other people's laundry is typically a job for the poor.*
© Peter Bruyneel

Cultural Contexts of Population Issues, Poverty and Inequality

High fertility increases poverty by slowing economic growth and by skewing the distribution of consumption against the poor. Reducing fertility – by reducing mortality, increasing education and improving access to services, especially reproductive health and family planning – counters both of these effects.[4] The Programme of Action of the International Conference on Population and Development (ICPD) is the basis for achieving population and development objectives within a framework of human rights and gender equality. Goals include universal access to reproductive health care, universal education and the empowerment of women and gender equality as decisive factors needed to facilitate development and reduce poverty. These goals have been incorporated in the Millennium Development Goals (MDGs).

Conditions of poverty and inequality, including women's unequal rights to household assets and decision-making, the burden of care that HIV and AIDS impose on women, and girls' and women's exposure to gender-based violence (including women who are refugees or victims of trafficking) make it more difficult to promote reproductive rights and health.

Population issues at the community, family and individual levels come down to decisions about the number of children to have and when to have them; decisions about health care and health-related behaviour; investments in children (often dependent on the gender of the child and anticipated future returns to the family); and decisions about whether and when to move in search of a better livelihood. All of these decisions are made within specific cultural contexts.

Culture and Fertility Issues

One of the most fundamental decisions a couple makes is whether, when and how many children to have. In the past, rigid societal and cultural constraints shaped childbearing behaviour; under-five mortality was high; and very high fertility was necessary for society's survival. This requirement became ossified in strict behavioural norms favouring numerous and closely spaced births. This remains true in situations where health care is poor, the cost of childrearing is relatively low and stable, children's

labour is an important economic asset for the family and there are no economic opportunities beyond subsistence farming. In these conditions, families reason that children can contribute to household welfare through child labour, agricultural work, domestic work and support for parents in old age. Where under-five mortality is high, higher fertility increases the likelihood that the desired number of children will survive.

Development redefines the value of children. More children survive, and their labour is no longer an important source of income for the family; on the contrary, parents wish to invest in their family's health and education. Cultural norms adapt, aided by increased exposure to reproductive health information and services.

Globally, the average number of children a woman has is 2.6; the number in developed countries is 1.6 and in less developed countries, 2.8. Income quintiles within countries also reflect fertility differentials. In each of the 48 countries where such data were gathered, women from the lower-income quintiles had consistently higher fertility than those in the highest-income quintiles (Figure 2). In sub-Saharan Africa and Latin America and the Caribbean,

Figure 2: Fertility differences between the rich and the poor

Average number of children by region and quintiles of household wealth

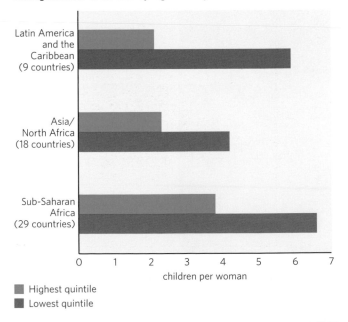

Source: Gwatkin, D.; Rutstein, S.; Johnson, K.; Suliman, E.; Wagstaff, A. and Amouzou, A. 2007. *Socio-Economic Differences in Health, Nutrition and Population Within Developing Countries: An Overview: Country Reports on HNP and Poverty.* Washington, D.C.: The World Bank.

poorer women had at least two children more than women in the higher-income quintiles. Women in the lower-income quintiles are also less likely to be using any method of contraception, even though they say they do not want any more children or that they do not want another one soon (Figure 3).

In every developing region of the world, the proportion of reproductive-age women who say they do not want another child (or do not want one soon) is higher among the wealthier quintiles than among those in the lower quintiles. The difference is particularly marked in Africa. Among women in the wealthier quintiles the proportion not using any method of contraception is lower than the corresponding proportion among poorer women. In other words, it is often maintained that poorer women have lower demand for contraception – they are more likely to want more children. Among those with demand, a higher proportion have an unmet need – they are less likely to have access to contraception. As smaller families become the norm, a larger share of observed fertility differences between rich and poor results from differences in access and use of contraception. The rich in poor countries have

both higher demand and greater ability to satisfy it. The poor desire larger families, in part because of residual cultural norms and in part because their circumstances have changed less. They do not get the signals about the changes in mortality levels and the returns on investments in education available to their wealthier compatriots.[5]

There are many reasons why women say they do not want any more children yet are still not using contraception. They may not have knowledge of family planning or access to it; but increased exposure to information and access to family planning services alone does not eliminate unmet need. Where cultural constraints have been taken into account, however, programmes to promote family planning have been more successful. One example is the rapid increase in contraceptive use among couples in the Islamic Republic of Iran and the ensuing decline in fertility rates. In 1989, the national family planning programme gained the support of high-ranking religious leaders who promoted smaller families in their weekly sermons as a social responsibility.[6]

While poorer women tend to have greater unmet need for family planning, there are instances where contracep-

Figure 3: Mean level of unmet need and total demand for family planning, by region and quintiles of household wealth

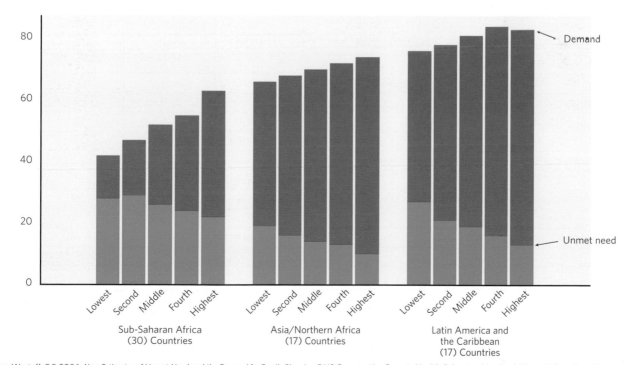

Source: Westoff, C.F. 2006. *New Estimates of Unmet Need and the Demand for Family Planning.* DHS Comparative Reports No. 14. Calverton, Maryland: Macro International Inc.

Note: Unweighted averages based on the most recent available survey for each country.

tive use has increased in the absence of economic development. In Bangladesh, for example, government commitment and intensive work by non-governmental organizations in securing local political and community-based support have led to increases in contraceptive use by low-income, illiterate women.[7]

Women with some information but little money, for example, in some poor, urban areas, may make decisions that they believe suit their circumstances but which might seem to be irrational and unhealthy. Rates of surgical contraception, especially among the poor, are very high. Ethnographic fieldwork revealed very high rates among low-income women in urban Brazil. Apparently this is a strategy to cope with increasing poverty rather than fertility regulation as such; apart from the pill, surgical contraception is the only method available.

Wealthier women, on the other hand, have access to a variety of methods through private clinics.[8]

Poverty and Health Care Delivery

Maternal mortality rates (MMR) mirror the huge discrepancies between the haves and the have-nots both within society and between countries:

- Poor women are far more likely to die as a result of pregnancy or childbirth.
- Poor families and individuals have less money and tend to live further away from health care facilities.
- Tackling maternal death and disability will reduce poverty.
- Investing in maternal health improves overall health service delivery. Maternal health indicators are used to gauge health system performance in terms of access, gender equity and institutional efficiency.[9]

Table 1: Estimates of MMR number of maternal deaths, lifetime risk, and range of uncertainty by United Nations MDG regions, 2005

Region	MMR (maternal deaths per 100,000) live births)*	Number of maternal deaths*	Lifetime risk of maternal death*: 1 in:	Range of uncertainty on MMR estimates	
				Lower estimate	Upper estimate
WORLD TOTAL	**400**	**536,000**	**92**	**220**	**650**
Developed regions**	9	960	7,300	8	17
Countries of the Commonwealth States (CIS)***	51	1,800	1,200	28	140
Developing Regions	450	533,000	75	240	730
Africa	820	276,000	26	410	1,400
Northern Africa****	160	5,700	210	85	290
Sub-Saharan Africa	900	270,000	22	450	1,500
Asia	330	241,000	120	190	520
Eastern Asia	50	9,200	1,200	31	80
South Asia	490	188,000	61	290	750
South-Eastern Asia	300	35,000	130	160	550
Western Asia	160	8,300	170	62	340
Latin America and the Caribbean	130	15,000	290	81	230
Oceania	430	890	62	120	1,200

Source: WHO, UNICEF, UNFPA and The World Bank. 2007. *Maternal Mortality in 2005*. Geneva: WHO.

* The MMR and lifetime risk have been rounded according to the following scheme: < 100, no rounding; 100–999, rounded to nearest 10; and >1,000, rounded to nearest 100. The numbers of maternal deaths have been rounded as follows: < 1,000, rounded to nearest 10, 1,000–9,999, rounded to nearest 100; and >10,000, rounded to nearest 1,000.

** Includes Albania, Australia, Austria, Belgium, Bosnia and Herzegovina, Bulgaria, Canada, Croatia, Czech Republic, Denmark, Estonia, Finland, France, Germany, Greece, Hungary, Iceland, Ireland, Italy, Japan, Latvia, Lithuania, Luxembourg, Malta, the Netherlands, New Zealand, Norway, Poland, Portugal, Romania, Serbia and Montenegro (Serbia and Montenegro became separate independent entities in 2006), Slovakia, Slovenia, Spain, Sweden, Switzerland, The former Yugoslav Republic of Macedonia, the United Kingdom, and the United States of America.

*** The CIS countries are Armenia, Azerbaijan, Belarus, Georgia, Kazakhstan, Kyrgyzstan, Tajikistan, Turkmenistan, Uzbekistan, the Republic of Moldova, the Russian Federation and Ukraine.

**** Excludes Sudan, which is included in sub-Saharan Africa.

Culture and Issues Related to Reproductive Health

In October 2007, the 62nd General Assembly of the United Nations approved a new target on universal access to reproductive health (following the recommendation of the 2005 World Summit). The indicators for measuring progress towards the target include providing access to family planning to reduce unintended pregnancies and to space intended pregnancies; addressing pregnancies of adolescents; and providing antenatal care to address health risks to mothers and children. Reproductive health problems remain the leading cause of ill health and death for women of childbearing age worldwide. The impact of reproductive health initiatives is to make motherhood safer by (1) improving access to family planning in order to reduce unintended pregnancies and achieve preferred spacing between intended pregnancies; (2) achieving skilled care for all births; and (3) providing timely obstetric care for all women who develop complications during childbirth.

SAFE MOTHERHOOD

Skilled care for all births, together with a range of interventions before, during and after pregnancy, is one of the keys to maternal health. Skilled birth attendants are accredited health professionals – midwives, doctors or nurses – with the skills to manage normal (uncomplicated) pregnancies, childbirth and the immediate post-natal period; to identify and manage complications in women and newborns; and to make referrals to appropriate emergency and obstetric care.[10] This definition excludes traditional birth attendants, trained or not. Antenatal care and delivery by a skilled birth attendant are more easily accessible and available to the better-off. In Africa, just 46.5 per cent of women have skilled birth attendants, in Asia, 65.4 per cent and in Latin America and the Caribbean, 88.5 per cent.[11] Data from 48 developing countries indicate that the proportion of women receiving antenatal care and the proportion of women giving birth with the assistance of a skilled birth attendant were consistently higher among high-income quintiles than the lowest quintiles (Figures 4 and 5). In sub-Saharan Africa, South Asia and South-Eastern Asia, the proportion of women giving birth with the assistance of a skilled birth attendant is more than twice as high among the wealthy than among poorer women.

Most women who use traditional birth attendants do not have access to trained birth attendants. But many

Figure 4: Availability of antenatal care

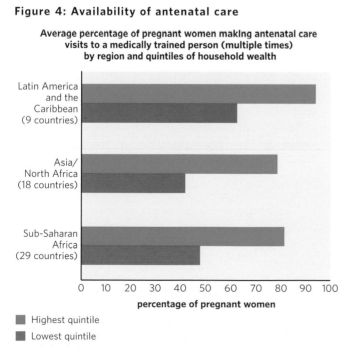

Average percentage of pregnant women making antenatal care visits to a medically trained person (multiple times) by region and quintiles of household wealth

■ Highest quintile
■ Lowest quintile

Source: Gwatkin, D. et. al. 2007. *Socio-economic differences in health, nutrition and population within developing countries*, Washington, D.C.: World Bank.

Figure 5: Births with skilled attendants

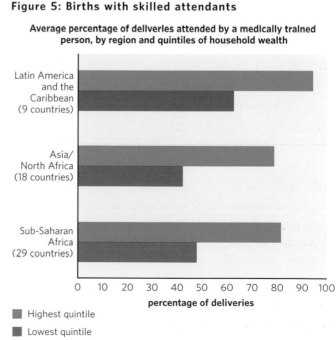

Average percentage of deliveries attended by a medically trained person, by region and quintiles of household wealth

■ Highest quintile
■ Lowest quintile

Source: WHO. 2007. "Proportion of Birth Attended by a Skilled Attendant—2007 Updates" *WHO Factsheet*. Geneva: World Health Organization.

LOCAL RESIDENCE DETERMINES THE EFFECTIVENESS OF AUXILIARY NURSE MIDWIVES

Research by Action Research and Training for Health (ARTH) in rural Rajasthan, India, revealed a correlation between the place of residence of the Auxiliary Nurse Midwives (ANMs) and their effectiveness. The majority (62 per cent) of the ANMs did not live in the villages where they worked because of poor living conditions, threats to their personal security and other factors. They found little demand for their services. The study concludes that improving the living and working conditions of the ANMs, and their own empowerment within the system, is essential for better maternal and child health care. Addressing the needs of first-line health care providers such as ANMs ensures good communication and trust, which in turn determine the quality of care. It also ensures their long-term participation and the sustainability of the programme.

Source: Action Research and Training for Health (ARTH). 2003. *Nurse Midwives for Maternal Health.* http://www.arth.in/publications.html, accessed June 2008.

Knowing the opposition and understanding its views can be the key to successful negotiations on sensitive issues such as adolescent information and service needs, and decision-making on fertility. Developing a different advocacy strategy for each stakeholder is often the most effective way to achieve consensus. For example, in Guatemala, advocacy, consultations and the involvement of as many actors as possible secured enactment of the Social Development Law in 2001.

In Iran, an initiative known as the "Women's Project" is mobilizing support for quality reproductive health services and the promotion of women's rights by providing research-based evidence, mounting public awareness campaigns and involving grass-roots communities. It builds capacity among institutions and organizations working in the social sector, and supports activities to empower women, including income-generating schemes. Prompted by a more open environment, religious leaders, community leaders and

choose traditional birth attendants because they assist in more than labour and the delivery of a child. They provide a variety of services ranging from physical care to advice on contraception, reproductive ailments and cures – before and after the birth. They are socially and emotionally connected to their clients, and are selected for the care and kindness they show, apart from their skill in birthing. These considerations should be part of the training of skilled birth attendants. For example, auxiliary nurse midwives who did not live in the communities they served found little demand for their services.

Gaining the confidence of women in rural households is the main reason the Government of Ethiopia has initiated a plan to train 2,800 women to become rural health extension workers. The plan, initiated in 2003, is "designed to improve the health status of families, with their full participation, using local technologies and the community's skill and wisdom".[12] Effective emergency obstetric care backup and referral can spark even faster reduction in maternal mortality.

Addressing the concerns of those opposed to information and services calls for advocacy and sensitive negotiation.

GUATEMALA: FINDING COMMON GROUND AND BUILDING ON IT

The Social Development Law of 2001 was made possible by broad political support for reducing one of the highest maternal mortality ratios in Latin America — 270 deaths per 100,000 live births. It adopts specific policies in the areas of population, reproductive health, family planning and sexuality education.

The Government and a number of stakeholders developed an elaborate advocacy strategy well in advance, including traditional supporters, potential allies within the Catholic and Evangelical churches and business leaders. There was broad consensus on the need to reduce maternal and infant mortality, which became the starting point for negotiations and the centrepiece of the new law.

Strategic partnerships helped gain support and reduce the influence of opposition groups. Articles on population and reproductive health ran in newspapers and magazines, and debates were aired on television and radio. UNFPA facilitated the process, supporting the government institutions and civil society organizations which assumed authorship and accountability for the new law.

Source: UNFPA. 2004. *Culture Matters: Working with Communities and Faith-based Organizations: Case Studies from Country Progammes.* New York: UNFPA.

▲ *Washing clothes in Madagascar. Without piped water, poor people have no choice but to use the same source for all their water needs – drinking, washing and sewage disposal.*

© Paula Bronstein

parliamentarians are now discussing protective legislation and other measures.

HIV AND AIDS

HIV and AIDS illustrate the contribution of economic inequalities in spreading infectious disease. HIV and AIDS cuts across social classes, but people who live in conditions of poverty are more vulnerable to infections, including HIV, and less likely to be treated. Loss of income and medical costs may drive a family into a new spiral of poverty. Caring for people living with HIV and AIDS increases the burden of women's unpaid workload and reduces their options for earning income. They may feel forced into high-risk work such as the sex industry. Caring for a growing number of orphans puts additional strain on the elderly and older siblings. This keeps children, especially girls, out of school, magnifying the intergenerational transmission of poverty and reducing potential economic growth.

There is no cure for AIDS and none is on the horizon; prevention remains critical for efforts to halt the epidemic.

Prevention efforts are taking hold in a number of countries. The downward trend in the number of new HIV infections in Côte d'Ivoire, Kenya, Zimbabwe, Cambodia, Myanmar and Thailand may be the result of scaled-up prevention.[13] Traditional leaders, indigenous and community elders, as well as faith-based organizations can be an important resource in the struggle to eliminate the spread of HIV, in countering stigma and in helping those affected and infected cope with economic and social hardship.

Migration, Immigrants and Cultural Diversity

MIGRATION, CULTURES AND CHOICE

In 2005, international migrants numbered 191 million, of whom nearly half were female.[14] Migration has been a mixed experience for both source and host communities and countries, and for migrants themselves. Migrants tend to fill the economic niches left by the local labour force, and migrants without qualifications or skills may find themselves in low-paid, unpleasant and often dangerous jobs. On the other hand, many migrants and their families have found opportunities for earning, investment, education and professional experience. Remittances to family members have helped reduce household poverty levels and contributed to economic growth. The figures have reached at least $251 billion annually.[15] According to one study, a one per cent increase in the share of remittances in a country's GDP leads to a 0.4 per cent decline in poverty.[16]

Remittances are much more than an economic phenomenon; they demonstrate how cultures – shared understandings and responses concerning family and communal responsibilities and obligations – can provide economic security for families.

Over time, migration encourages cultural shifts, as some migrants broaden their identities, attach less significance to some of the belief systems and norms within their old communities, and perhaps begin to contest some of them. Migrants transmit change through contact from abroad and by returning home with new ways of thinking and making sense of reality. Individuals can be influential – rock stars and football players, political dissidents and successful entrepreneurs send powerful cultural messages. Migration stimulates cultural shifts in host countries as well, as people absorb new ideas and approaches from other countries. Through routes such as these, cultures encompass different approaches to issues, including human rights and gender equality. Much depends on the character of these wider contexts, and on individual migrants' experience in host societies and in their home countries.

Some migrants enrich their world view by exposure to different cultures; others remain focused on the discrimination and hostility they face. Economic perceptions, such as migrants' poverty or wealth, competition for jobs with the local population or economic dependence, may bolster social barriers and deepen misunderstanding. Host populations sometimes hold migrants responsible for a variety of economic and social ills, whether poverty in South Africa or social disruption in Italy.

Host countries' migration policies can promote integration, strategies to manage diversity and cross-cultural learning. Civil society can assist by dispelling myths and quelling rumours, providing migrants with knowledge of and access to certain services, and engaging their participation in integration processes. Source countries have to contend with losing not only skills but key family and community members even while they may gain overseas cultural interlocutors. Social and economic policies have to protect the families of migrants and the interests of workers going overseas, especially women.

Trafficking is the dark underside of migration, damaging communities of origin and destination as well as the individuals concerned. Opening national borders and international markets has increased legal flows of capital, goods and labour across borders, but it has also globalized organized crime. Improved information technologies and transportation allow transnational syndicates to operate easily. Those who fall into the hands of traffickers are drawn by the chance of a better life or forced by friends or relatives. They may be duped by false promises, or simply sold. Increasingly restrictive immigration policies in Europe and North America are driving more and more

▲ Eight-year-old Hajira at the door of a battery recycling workshop in Bangladesh. She works with her mother and looks after the younger children, too.
© Shehzad Noorani/Getty Images

would-be migrants into the hands of traffickers. Trafficked women find themselves forced into prostitution, sex tourism or commercial marriages, or into unpaid or poorly paid domestic, agricultural or sweatshop labour.[17]

INTERNAL MIGRATION

Migration from rural areas as well as natural increase are responsible for the rapid increase in urban population in recent decades. Both migrants and the non-migrant urban poor are greatly disadvantaged. Compared to other poor urban residents, the reproductive health care needs of migrants may have more to do with their insecurity in respect to employment, livelihood and social networks than with medical or health services as such.[18] Although repro-

ductive health-care services may be easier to reach in urban areas than in rural areas, many urban migrants cannot afford to use them. Urban migrants' lack of social contacts also works against their access to and use of emergency obstetric and gynaecological care in hospitals. Poor migrant women in Rajasthan, for example, return to their homes in the village to give birth,[19] even though emergency obstetric and gynaecological care, child immunization and postnatal care are likely to be less accessible than in the city.

CONTEXTS AND COMPLEXITIES

Lifestyles and expectations are rapidly changing. As geographical and social mobility increases, relationships and the extent of shared experience among family members and communities also change. Changes in social and economic opportunities are altering people's expectations and desires for their families. The accumulating impact of social change is creating the conditions whereby cultural shifts take place.

As cultures impact on the context within which policies take place, the various elements that make up culture are also transformed. Cultural meanings, norms and practices are, therefore, not immutable. They shift and change as individuals and groups acquire new information, gain capabilities and are exposed to different contexts. Throughout, cultural sensitivity remains a key ingredient for policies that seek to deal with the challenges of migration and urbanization – wherever those intersect with gender relations and human rights dynamics.

Negotiating Culture: Gender and Reproductive Health in Conflict Situations

6

Since the end of the Cold War, most armed conflicts have been within rather than between States. Between 1998 and 2007, there were 34 major armed conflicts – all but three internal – and about four times that many armed conflicts in total.[1] Far more civilians than soldiers become casualties in these conflicts,[2] many of them women and girls.

Armed conflict threatens women's rights – including reproductive rights – and health, and can exacerbate culturally rooted gender inequalities. Women also occupy different roles in wartime, some as combatants, and many fill the spaces in economic and political life left by men. Culturally sensitive approaches can help development practitioners mitigate some of the ill effects of conflict, minimize deterioration in gender relations and work with local communities and relevant stakeholders to protect whatever progress has been made towards gender equality, including women's rights and reproductive health. These approaches can also help to ensure that women become important players in negotiation processes, and are integrated in post-conflict rehabilitation and reconstruction efforts.

Cultures, Gender Relations and Armed Conflicts

Much of the work on relationships between cultures and gender in conflict situations challenges conventional perceptions of men's and women's roles. Many cultures regard women as "mothers" and "guardians of the culture", traditionally passive and in need of male protection. Men and boys, seen as inherently aggressive, are usually enlisted for wars, although in some societies women are involved as combatants as well as in civilian roles. Men are normally the primary targets in war and are usually most of the casualties, but sexual violence is also a tactic of warfare. Women are seen as the protectors of children – the future – and bearers of the cultural heritage – the past – of a nation or community. This makes

There is increasing awareness in the development field that longstanding cultural norms regarding the identity and role of women in society are a significant barrier to the full enjoyment of women's rights. The social restrictions that result from these norms are often exacerbated during armed conflict.[3]

◀ *Women's exposure to all kinds of violence increases in wartime, including violence from their partners.*
© UNFPA

them targets for attack. "The rape of women in conflict situations is intended not only as violence against women, but as an act of aggression against a nation or community."[4]

Their communities may offer some sympathy to women who suffer violence, but may also regard them as tainted and worthless. The men in their families, feeling the shame of failing to "protect their women", may subject them to further violence. Because many cultures see gender-based violence as a private issue and may even see it as normal, they do not recognize or confront it.

As a result, women rarely discuss sexual violence against them, even though it may have occurred in public view. For example, women in Kosovo, Croatia, and Bosnia and Herzegovina refused to report the sexual abuse they experienced during the war for fear of stigmatization by their communities.[5]

Men are also victims of rape. Male rape can be even more deeply shaming than female rape; therefore, "undermining men's sense of masculinity becomes a key channel for men to exercise power over other men".[6] Men will rarely admit to suffering rape.

Militarization can impact on cultures by sharpening perceptions and misperceptions of existing gender roles. Militarization calls for a show of aggressive masculinity, which may involve misogyny:

> *The language of armies often reflects this construction of masculinity, as the most common insults are those that suggest that a soldier is homosexual or feminine. The misogyny of armies is intertwined with both homophobia and racism. Both women and members of ethnic minorities who enter the military are frequently subjected to sexual and racial harassment.[7]*

Sexual violence was a by-product of the collapse of social order in Kenya brought on by the post-election conflict; but it was also a tool to terrorize individuals and families, and precipitate their flight. Anecdotal reports from all regions, in particular Mombasa, Nairobi, and parts of the North Rift, told of threats of sexual violence as a tactic to instil fear: women were told to vacate their property or they and their children would be raped. Women were further threatened in the temporary shelters to which they fled; women in houses in Timboroa, for example, were told to move or risk rape.[8]

Armed conflict imposes other costs on gender relations. Forced displacement disrupts families. Women's burdens grow heavier because they become responsible for households, with less access to resources. As women assume leadership for families, gender roles change. This could prompt cultural changes, but men may instead respond with violence against women.[9] In these fragile and resource-poor conditions, women and girls may try to earn money or merely a little food from sex work, including with men from occupying forces. Families may resent these practices, and men may respond with violence, often leading to family upheavals. HIV and AIDS are spreading in conflict zones as sexual practices change. The disease brings additional stigma and is not openly discussed.

Addressing Gender Relations in Armed Conflicts: United Nations Security Council Resolution 1325 (2000)

United Nations Security Council (UNSC) resolution 1325, adopted in October 2000,[10] was the product of intense advocacy from a number of women's and peace organizations. Despite recognition by the Fourth World Conference on Women, there was resistance to the proposition that women's human rights were an international security concern. UNSC resolution 1325, together with the Windhoek Declaration, 2000[11] establish that gender issues are pertinent to international peace and security. UNSC resolution 1325 is clear in its denunciation of human rights abuses. It takes a firm position on the importance of women's inclusion and participation in peace negotiations and peacebuilding, despite existing cultural practices. Resolution 1325 also recognizes that its provisions can only be realized through cultural engagement, which requires "…measures that support local women's peace initiatives and indigenous processes for conflict resolution, and that involve women in all of the implementation mechanisms of the peace agreements".

There are a number of concerns about progress on UNSC resolution 1325. First, while the resolution is a landmark, there are questions about the extent to which it incorporates men's and women's issues, as opposed to focusing largely on women and girls, and offers guidance on a gendered approach.[12] Second, progress reviews indicate that implementation requires confronting cultural obstacles within development organizations and building technical expertise among staff.[13] It also requires agreement, at the highest levels, "that the issue of women, peace and security is consistent with the fundamental purpose of security institutions".[14] Third, without culturally sensitive gendered approaches, "peace interventions" may fail to recognize and support the cultural shifts that could culminate in more equitable gender relations. They may inadvertently prop up the very structures and relations that the resolution aims to challenge. Analysts observe:

1. Gender power imbalances are entrenched within public and private institutions, including governmental and non-governmental development organizations that intervene to end armed conflict and build peace.[15]

25 RAPE AS A WEAPON OF WAR

"[Women who were] raped during the war tell their close friends. You hardly hear of women coming out in public to talk about all those things that happened to them. They would rather suffer in silence until they can get over it. They try to live with it or live with the idea that it didn't happen to them alone. If hundreds of other girls can live with it, you can also live with it and, gradually, it vanishes away ... but most of the raping was done in the open. A particular rebel may like your daughter, and right in front of you – the mum, the dad, the other sisters and brothers – it will be done openly. So that was how many girls got to know that their friends were raped."

Source: Bennett, O., Bexley, J. and Warnock, K. 1996. *Arms to Fight, Arms to Protect: Women Speak Out About Conflict*, p. 39. London: Panos Publications.

26 WOMEN ATTACKED: SURVIVORS CARRY EXTRA BURDENS

DARFUR, Sudan — Since the conflict began in the Darfur region of western Sudan in 2003, over 200,000 people have been killed and more than two million have been displaced. Altogether, some four million people are in need of humanitarian aid and protection. Violence against civilians, much of it against women, has been a feature of the conflict. Thousands of women have been raped. Villages have been burned to the ground and destroyed, forcing their inhabitants to flee, often with just the clothes on their backs. With their villages destroyed, many families have lived for years on the run, in informal settlements or in internal refugee camps throughout Darfur. Many women have become primary caretakers for other survivors, their responsibilities compounded by the loss of husbands and livelihoods and the need to find essentials for family survival.

Source: UNFPA. 2007. "Dispatches from Darfur: Caring for the Ones who Care for Others." New York: UNFPA. http://www.unfpa.org/news/news.cfm?ID=1026, accessed April 2008.

2. Humanitarian interventions make impartial assessments of victims' needs and interests, but risk being gender-blind in their delivery. The interventions of humanitarian groups often demonstrate a lack of sensitivity to gender.[16]

3. Although long-term interventions aimed at the social and economic integration of women can greatly improve gender relations, long-term development assistance has decreased while funding for complex humanitarian emergencies has increased proportionately.... There is even less money now for long-term development assistance, and where it is available gender equality becomes a considerably lower priority.[17]

4. Humanitarian aid agencies and States often shy away from challenging gender-based violence.[18]

5. Disarmament, demobilization and reintegration programmes need to develop more culturally sensitive gendered approaches.

6. Generally, women are assumed to be lacking in the expertise to function in the public arena and are excluded from peace-making processes. This underrepresentation also extends to peacekeeping and peacebuilding institutions.

Excerpt from *Displaced and Desperate: Assessment of Reproductive Health for Colombia's Internally Displaced Persons.* London: Marie Stopes International, February 2003.

"Two million Colombians have fled armed conflict and persecution: many of them have been uprooted and displaced repeatedly over the past 15 years. As the war continues to escalate, some people are displaced en masse, but the majority flee as individuals and families, and do not want to acknowledge their displaced status for fear of retribution. Many of the displaced are indigenous groups uprooted from rural to urban areas and forced to flee again from one urban *barrio* to another in search of security and survival.... Internally displaced people (IDPs), particularly women, girls and adolescents, experience horrendous reproductive health problems in Colombia. Gender-based violence (GBV), including rape followed by murder, sexual servitude, forced contraception and abortions, is perpetrated by armed actors, is extensive and is largely unaddressed. In addition to GBV inflicted by armed actors, the situation is desperate for some families; the team heard of some instances of girls and boys being sexually exploited by their parents or turning to prostitution for family survival needs. The assessment team learned from IDP women that domestic violence is a major problem, exacerbated by the difficult living situation for IDPs.

"The prevalence of sexually transmitted infections (STIs) among IDPs is unknown but anecdotal reports from government and UNFPA representatives suggest that it is very high. In some indigenous communities, health providers, unable to reach men for adequate treatment, have admitted pregnant women to the hospital to prevent them from becoming re-infected and to prevent mother-to-child transmission. This mobile population living among armed actors and on the whole without access to medical care is in danger of an explosion of STIs, including HIV.

"The circumstances for adolescent IDPs [are] dire, and very little is being done to recognize their specific needs and capacities. Unable to cope with their circumstances or enticed by drug traffickers infiltrating urban barrios, many young boys turn to drugs, alcohol and theft. Some adolescent girls seek solace and comfort in motherhood, while others would prefer to avoid or delay pregnancy, suggesting a need, currently unmet, for family planning. A recent study by Profamilia indicated that 30 per cent of adolescent IDPs were already mothers or pregnant with their first child, a percentage nearly twice that of adolescents in Colombia's general population in 2000."

Source: http://www.womenscommission.org/pdf/co_rh.pdf, accessed March 2008.

Culturally Sensitive Approaches, Gender Relations and Armed Conflicts

Culturally sensitive approaches are especially critical in contexts of armed conflicts. They are important for addressing the gaps in policy that United Nations Security Council resolution 1325 outlines, as well as those noted in concerns expressed about the progress on the resolution.

CULTURALLY SENSITIVE APPROACHES ARE ESSENTIAL FOR UNDERSTANDING MEN AND WOMEN'S EXPERIENCES IN ARMED CONFLICTS.

There is sufficient evidence that social constructions of masculinity can worsen gender relations during periods of war. For example, some analysts argue that violence against women in northern Uganda was in some cases the outcome of feelings of emasculation and frustration:

men's experiences do not match cultural expectations of masculinity, which require that they provide for the material needs of their wives and children, as well as physical protection. War worsens the already poor structural conditions. Unable to fulfil their expected roles, men take out their frustrations on the women whom they have failed: "It is generally assumed that women differ from men, that they are weaker, incapable, a burden, a position legitimized by the biblical story in Genesis that man was created first, woman from his rib, and the saying that women are the weaker vessels...."[19]

Similarly, focus groups among women in camps in Kenya revealed that domestic violence increased during conflicts as men, frustrated by lack of employment, cramped living conditions, inability to provide for their families, women's lack of desire for sex and other challenges, punished women and children for their own unease.[20]

28 UNSC RESOLUTION 1325 (2000):

Expresses concern that civilians, particularly women and children, account for the vast majority of those adversely affected by armed conflict, including as refugees and internally displaced persons, and increasingly are targeted by combatants and armed elements, and [recognizes] the consequent impact this has on durable peace and reconciliation,

Reaffirms the important role of women in the prevention and resolution of conflicts and in peace-building, and stressing the importance of their equal participation and full involvement in all efforts for the maintenance and promotion of peace and security, and the need to increase their role in decision-making with regard to conflict prevention and resolution,

Reaffirms also the need to implement fully international humanitarian and human rights law that protects the rights of women and girls during and after conflicts,

Emphasizes the need for all parties to ensure that mine clearance and mine awareness programmes take into account the special needs of women and girls,

Recognizes the urgent need to mainstream a gender perspective into peacekeeping operations, and in this regard noting the Windhoek Declaration and the Namibia Plan of Action on Mainstreaming a Gender Perspective in Multidimensional Peace Support Operations (S/2000/693),

Recognizes also the importance of the recommendation contained in the statement of its President to the press of 8 March 2000 for specialized training for all peacekeeping personnel on the protection, special needs and human rights of women and children in conflict situations,

Recognizes that an understanding of the impact of armed conflict on women and girls, effective institutional arrangements to guarantee their protection, and full participation in the peace process can significantly contribute to the maintenance and promotion of international peace and security,

The resolution, therefore, calls on Member States "to ensure increased representation of women at all decision-making levels in national, regional and international institutions and mechanisms for the prevention, management, and resolution of conflict; encourages the Secretary-General to ... call for an increase in the participation of women at decision-making [and operational] levels in conflict resolution and peace processes; expresses its willingness to incorporate a gender perspective into peacekeeping operations and urges the Secretary-General to ensure that, where appropriate, field operations include a gender component, [including by ensuring that training is provided]."

The resolution calls on all actors involved, when negotiating and implementing peace agreements, to adopt a gender perspective, including, *inter alia*: (a) The special needs of women and girls during repatriation and resettlement and for rehabilitation, reintegration and post-conflict reconstruction; (b) Measures that support local women's peace initiatives and indigenous processes for conflict resolution, and that involve women in all of the implementation mechanisms of the peace agreements; (c) Measures that ensure the protection of and respect for human rights of women and girls, particularly as they relate to the constitution, the electoral system, the police and the judiciary. It also calls upon all parties to armed conflict to respect fully international law applicable to the rights and protection of women and girls as civilians ... [and] to take special measures to protect women and girls from gender-based violence, particularly rape and other forms of sexual abuse, and all other forms of violence in situations of armed conflict. It emphasizes the responsibility of all States to put an end to impunity and to prosecute those responsible for genocide, crimes against humanity, war crimes including those relating to sexual violence against women and girls, and in this regard, stresses the need to exclude these crimes, where feasible, from amnesty provisions. [Additionally, it] calls upon all parties to armed conflict to respect the civilian and humanitarian character of refugee camps and settlements, and to take into account the particular needs of women and girls, including in their design, and recalls its resolution 1208 of 19 November 1998; and encourages all those involved in the planning for disarmament, demobilization and reintegration to consider the different needs of female and male ex-combatants and to take into account the needs of their dependants.

RECONSTRUCTION AND TRANSFORMATION

A particularly effective programme was developed in Central America to help an estimated 45,000 Guatemalans who fled a civil war in the 1980s and sought refuge in Mexico. When women demanded a voice in negotiations to return home, UNHCR funded projects to develop women's rights, combat their illiteracy and improve health services and leadership skills.

Women were directly involved in repatriation negotiations, and among the concessions they won was recognition, for the first time, of the principle of equal ownership of both private and communal property. Although it took a decade of work, it is enshrined in Guatemalan jurisprudence, benefiting the entire population.

Source: http://www.unhcr.org/publ/PUBL/3e2d4d5511.pdf, accessed August 2008.

Profemme Twese Hamwe is a women's collective formed in Rwanda in 1993. Through its peace and reconciliation programmes, it has made a substantial contribution to rebuilding society in Rwanda, following the 1994 genocide. One of the organization's major objectives is to facilitate "the structural transformation of Rwandan society by putting into place the political, material, economic and moral conditions favourable for the rehabilitation of social justice and equal opportunity, to build a real and durable peace." In addition, Profemme Twese Hamwe helps to build capacity among women through communication, information and education.

Source: www.profemme.org.rw, accessed August 2008.

Since the 2003 invasion of Iraq, women have contributed significantly to reconstruction and to maintaining social stability. A variety of women's associations have flourished to address practical needs and to provide for education and training and income generation.

Source: Al-Ali, N. 2007. "Iraqi Women: Four Years After the Invasion." Silver City, New Mexico, and Washington, D.C.: Foreign Policy In Focus. http://fpif.org/fpiftxt/4055. Accessed August 2008.

Though women are often portrayed as vulnerable and victimized, Ethiopian women have had a long history of being involved in resisting invading forces, maintaining societies during periods of armed conflict and contributing to peacebuilding and post-conflict rehabilitation.

Source: Mulugeta Tefera, E. 2005. "The Invincible Invisibles: Ethiopian Women in Conflict and Peacemaking." Addis Ababa: University for Peace.

This knowledge demonstrates the need for livelihood opportunities in addition to strategies for exposing, challenging and changing the cultural perceptions, norms and practices that underpin gender inequalities and gender-based violence; and the need for other psychosocial initiatives that deal with how men and women perceive themselves and their roles.

Culturally sensitive approaches recognize that men and women exercise power in varied and unexpected ways and that these variations are important for understanding how cultures – shared understandings or systems of meaning – shift and change; what types of culturally sensitive policies are needed for promoting human rights and the spaces that exist, or may be

According to women in Mombasa, "When sexual desire has gone down, physical violence goes up." Other women agreed that in the camps, a father "is as good as a child" and "when the husband is not working, he becomes part of the children," for whom the women are responsible. In at least three camps, incidents of domestic violence requiring police intervention had already been noted.[21]

emerging, for change. For example, the common perception of women as victims and men as aggressors does not always describe what happens during wars.[22] It is now well established that women, as in Liberia, may take part in combat, and that not all men are aggressors. Women have taken part in independence struggles, for example, but this has not automatically translated into equal opportunities and access to decision-making positions once the conflict is over. Recognition of these variations is important for checking popular representations of men's and women's roles in armed and post-conflict situations as well as the unfortunate labelling of people's capacities. This has, in turn, important policy implications.

Assumptions of vulnerability are often used to justify top-down,

THE GIRL CHILD AND ARMED CONFLICT: RECOGNIZING AND ADDRESSING GRAVE VIOLATIONS OF GIRLS' HUMAN RIGHTS

During armed conflict, girls are subject to widespread and, at times, systematic forms of human rights violations that have mental, emotional, spiritual, physical and material repercussions. These violations include illegal detention with or without family members, abduction and forced removal from families and homes, disappearances, torture and other inhuman treatment, amputation and mutilation, forced recruitment into fighting forces and groups, slavery, sexual exploitation, increased exposure to HIV and AIDS, and a wide range of physical and sexual violations, including rape, enforced pregnancy, forced prostitution, forced marriage and forced childbearing.

There is urgent need for better documentation, monitoring and reporting on the extreme suffering that armed conflict inflicts on girls, as well as on the many roles girls play during conflict and its aftermath. Such information and response mechanisms are needed for the purpose of strengthening and developing policy and programs to prevent and/or address these grave rights violations.

Source: Paper prepared by Mazurana, D. and K. Carlson for the United Nations Division for the Advancement of Women and UNICEF's Expert Group Meeting on the Elimination of all Forms of Discrimination and Violence Against the Girl Child, Florence: 25-28 September 2008.

"In all wars and disasters, it is persons with disabilities that are first to die; persons with disabilities that are the first to get disease and infection; and it is persons with disabilities who are the last to get resources and medicines when they are handed out. They are treated as the bottom of the pile."[24]

A. IDENTIFYING SPECIFIC NEEDS

Culturally based discrimination against women, girls, minorities and those with disabilities may be intensified during wartime, and even the most serious violations may go unchecked. In the Democratic Republic of the Congo, men targeted Batwa women for sex, believing that if a man had sex with a Batwa woman, he would be cured of HIV and protected from death by bullets, and that his spinal cord could never be broken. Some of these women were captured and kept as sexual slaves, and some were cannibalized.[25] In the Basilan region of the Philippines, violence against women escalated during the period of conflict from 2000 to 2003. Their communities considered raped women unclean, and they were forced to marry the soldiers who had raped them.[26]

People with disabilities, particularly women and children, can suffer significantly worse forms of human rights abuses in wartime. Over 80 per cent of the estimated 600 million people living with disabilities live in developing countries, and large numbers have been displaced by armed conflict. With cultural knowledge and engagement, their experiences are identified and more tailored interventions constructed.[27]

B. PROVIDING URGENT SERVICES

Cultural knowledge is critical for providing emergency sexual and reproductive health services to refugees and other populations during periods of war. With cultural knowledge, external agencies can help providers identify needs, the channels most likely to be effective and the essential partnerships.

Women's unique health needs, including all aspects of sexual and reproductive health, become more difficult to meet in wartime. The inadequacy or absence of obstetric

---

needs-assessment interventions, which can "blind the aid administrator to the resilience and resourcefulness" of people affected by armed conflicts and "limit livelihood and reconstruction options".[23] Conversely, knowledge of who people are, how they make sense of their lives, how they work to tame armed conflicts, how they deliver services, and what has changed as a result of the conflict is indispensable for locating and supporting local initiatives and indigenous processes.

Impact, Analysis, Response

People's experience during armed conflict depends on factors such as ethnicity, race, gender, class, age, faith and culture. Culturally sensitive approaches are important for understanding how these "intersectionalities" play out, analysing the impact of armed conflict on different categories of people, and responding with policies focused on specific needs.

Because they relate to such an intimate sphere of life, reproductive health interventions must be delivered with great care and cultural sensitivity. Programmes must be particularly sensitive to religious and ethical values and cultural backgrounds of the refugee population. Providing comprehensive reproductive care also often requires careful coordination among several agencies.[28]

services, contraception or protection from sexually transmitted infection can threaten women's health and survival. Stress, inadequate nutrition and poor hygiene compromise pregnancy and delivery. The risk of sexual violence and exploitation increases.

It is critical to provide immediate and effective emergency services and supplies, including basic obstetric care. Working with individuals and groups in the heart of the conflict is important for success. Front-line agencies should be aware of women's specific needs for reproductive health care, and target them deliberately as partners in service delivery. Health-care providers need awareness and training to ensure the best possible perinatal care; availability of condoms and other contraceptives; voluntary HIV counselling and testing, during which HIV prevention is stressed; measures to prevent transmission of HIV from mother to baby; as well as post-partum care designed to substantially reduce the number of maternal deaths. Beyond providing supplies and supporting facilities, UNFPA-supported programmes emphasize life skills education, including information for women and girls on how to protect themselves against sexually transmitted infections such as HIV, and specialized information and support for adolescents. UNFPA also develops a broad range of alliances with government, humanitarian agencies and local organizations to provide services, including psychological support, to survivors of sexual violence.[29]

Young Guatemalan girl at the end of a brief civil war. ▶
© Leonard Mccombe//Getty Images

C. BUILDING EFFECTIVE PARTNERSHIPS

Culturally sensitive approaches are crucial for building effective partnerships, particularly during periods of war. For example, Catholic Relief Services (CRS) has been supporting inter-religious dialogue in order to promote peacebuilding. In the Mindanao area of the Philippines, the organization has been working to facilitate dialogue between Christian and Muslim leaders. In Pakistan, CRS has been using the teachings of Islam and Christianity to encourage forgiveness, peacebuilding and reconciliation. In addition, CRS supported a millennial inter-faith peace walk in Pakistan, and, in Cameroon, it is supporting citizen education, conflict resolution and peacebuilding programmes.[30] Similarly, Islamic Relief Services is collaborating with the Catholic Agency for Overseas Development (CAFOD) to support children in the Gaza Strip who are traumatized by violence.[31] In northern Uganda,

Freedom to express cultural identity can be a powerful way to maintain a community's mental and physical health. Freedom of expression is also a right and, as our language of assistance moves from needs-based to rights-based, respect for the empowering forms of cultural expression should inform our thinking and planning.[32]

For all populations – those women who remain in their war-torn communities, those who return to their communities after being displaced and those forced to flee – the most effective psychosocial programmes work within the culture or across cultures to provide services that re-establish and strengthen community ties destroyed by war and displacement.[35]

Anglican, Catholic, Muslim and Orthodox religious leaders have formed the Acholi Religious Leaders' Peace Initiative to facilitate reconciliation in terms that people will understand and respect culturally. This has had unintended benefits: "In the past, it was difficult to get an Anglican reverend like me together with a sister from the Catholic Church…. But right now, the local religious leaders are working together, and that alone is a very big step."[33]

Partnerships are important for providing critical psychosocial support to victims of sexual violence. This involves working with health-care providers, the police and legislators so that survivors can be treated with the care that is rightfully theirs. Beyond this, it calls for alliances with advocates of legal reform, who aim for better policing and stringent punishment for violators. It also entails tackling gender relations, for example, ensuring that women have appropriate and influential positions in the design of humanitarian assistance, peacekeeping and peacebuilding.

Given the depth of cultural opposition to women in leadership, this can be an enormous challenge. The experience of an array of women's organizations and women leaders working in these harsh environments shows that peace agreements, post-conflict reconstruction, governance and security are more effective when

women participate; but these processes still rarely include women.[36]

Women are critical partners in all successful programmes, not only as leaders but in helping each other, often in ways not open to external actors. In the IDP camps of South Darfur, for example, UNFPA is supporting centres which are "safe zones" where women meet and share their knowledge and their experiences with health and violence issues.

"Women are coming here to talk about their problems," Awatif says. *"When you are just one person, it is your problem alone. When you tell [your problems] to a lot of women, it becomes all of their problems."*[37]

D. RECOVERING CULTURE, RECOVERING SELF

Development organizations have found that the ability to express cultural identities may help people recover from the trauma of war: "Enabling displaced people to retain all that remains of their distinct personhood may be vital for their future, for their health, for holding them together as a community, and for maintaining or restoring their dignity after the trauma of exile."[38] Practitioners explain that beyond encouraging people to express their culture, drawing on the cultural expressions that people know and understand can make services more effective. For example,

Culturally-informed psychosocial interventions that improve women's social networks and economic opportunities contribute to the sense of calm and stability that must exist before we can truly address and resolve the horrors experienced in conflict, and assist women and their communities in moving toward a peaceful future.[34]

In mid-March hundreds of Congolese women, men and girls raised banners that read: "Together, let us say No to the silence, for the dignity of the Congolese" and "Enough sexual violence!" With faces of determination, the women, men and girls waved these slogans high above their heads. More than 1,000 Congolese authorities and civilians, UN leaders, NGOs and civil society groups were gathered in Kinkole, a suburb of Kinshasa, to kick off a nationwide public awareness campaign aimed to eradicate an epidemic of sexual violence. An average of 1,100 rape cases are reported each month, according to UNFPA, "Sexual violence constitutes a plague in the DRC," said Dr. Margaret Agama, the UNFPA representative in the country. "Initially, rape was used as a tool of war by all the belligerent forces involved in the country's recent conflicts, but now sexual violence is unfortunately not only perpetrated by armed factions but also by ordinary people occupying positions of authority, neighbours, friends and family members."

In January, the signing of a peace deal officially ended the conflicts that have raged in the country for a decade. Thus, the campaign organized by UNFPA along with the national Ministry of Women, Family and Children came at an important time, as communities work to rebuild infrastructures and re-integrate over 1 million people displaced by the conflicts. The campaign raised the level of awareness on sexual violence throughout the national and international communities and united authorities, neighbours, survivors, friends and family members in its elimination.... The need to end impunity is a main message in the UNFPA-led campaign and has also become a key agenda for the country's leaders. In February, the Congolese Minister for Women, Family and Protection of the Child, Philomène Omatuku, declared to the public, "I would say from now on that we women of the DRC, we say no to sexual violence, no to impunity. The Congolese women require peace."

The intensive, multi-faceted campaign to raise awareness and sensitize key actors at all levels took place in the 11 provinces of the DRC for one month. A wide range of communication channels – including media outlets, theatre, open telephone lines, films and video forums and debates – were being used to reach out to all, including the Government and the diplomatic community. The campaign also relied on the authority of recognized moral community leaders to influence public opinion.

Source: http://www.unfpa.org/news/news.cfm? ID=1113, accessed June 2008.

---

the United Nations Children's Fund (UNICEF) has used art, drama, music and dance to help displaced children recover in places as different as Kosovo, Colombia, Sri Lanka, Algeria, Croatia and Rwanda.[39] The most effective strategy for helping Sudanese women refugees is to strengthen communities and build social and cultural networks. In Afghanistan, practitioners advise against using Western-based diagnoses and treatments to alleviate traumas suffered by women in conflict. Instead, they suggest that cultural fluency (knowing the language of the culture) is important for understanding what women have gone through and what they need to recover.[40] In Aceh Province, Indonesia, displaced women require support that incorporates their Muslim faith and recognizes cultural approaches to grieving. Acehnese women believe that prolonged grieving holds back their loved ones' souls from reaching God; they want practical help such as education and training to build their futures, not lengthy discussions of trauma and grief. Only culturally sensitive approaches can uncover and respond to such particularities of need.

Negotiating Cultures Within Development Organizations

Cultural awareness and engagement are as important in development organizations themselves as in their national and local working contexts. Staff members' own cultural perceptions may affect their approaches to their work. Culturally sensitive approaches demand attention to the ways in which interventions aimed at conflict prevention, humanitarian assistance, peacekeeping and peacebuilding influence gender relations and culture.

UNFPA, for instance, is working to build an organizational culture ready to respond to human rights abuses and promote gender equality in conflict situations. Through its work, it has found that the most effective interventions emerge through dialogue, developing strategic partnerships with people committed to change and building on local initiatives. Development workers in their own societies normally have intimate knowledge of what is practicable at different points in time; they know about the processes required for change and the tools and methods most likely to work. However, strategic partnerships require commitment and time. They develop best where everyone in the partnership recognizes that people have different ways of thinking and deserve mutual recognition and respect. Development agencies are increasingly finding and using the most effective symbols and forms of communication for transmitting messages in different cultures. Rather than convey agency-conceptualized messages about behaviour change, agencies engage with communities, using varied cultural forms of communication such as songs, dance and

We have taken the lessons to strengthen working relationships with communities and local social, political, cultural and religious leaders, engaging them in dialogue, listening to them, sharing knowledge and insights, jointly planning the way forward and moving ahead. UNFPA is set on a path of systematically mainstreaming cultural factors in programming efforts in order to make greater progress and affirm human rights.

—Thoraya Ahmed Obaid, Executive Director, UNFPA

drama to open conversations and involve people in building strategies for tackling rights abuses and promoting gender equality in ways suited to their contexts.

32 MEN'S LEADERSHIP PROGRAMME

"My name is Kayembe Tshibangu, head of Mushumune Commune in Bagira, Bukavu city. I am a father of five. I was a normal man, living with my family in a normal way. I behaved like every man within the society. My wife was a slave to me, she had no rights and had to respect me absolutely. She was always in the home, and could not go out to meet other women. She belonged to me, because at our marriage, I paid a bride-price — the dowry, which gave me all the authority to treat her as I wished. She was at my mercy for sexual activity, anytime, anyplace, anywhere. Refusal went with punishment. I was a complete tyrant in my home. When I arrived at home the children and everyone ran away, because the 'lion' had arrived. It was a complete and absolute dictatorship. This was because I did not know any alternative way of living.

"After 18th August 2005, the day of encounter with the Men's Leadership Program of Women for Women International, things changed completely. I was converted and took on a new life. Even my children and family asked what had happened to me. They could not believe it. It was too good to be true! They thought it was a dream, and it would go away after some time, like a mirage. No, never again will I go back to my old self. My family members and I are now friends, comrades. We talk and laugh together, and there is peace in the home. No more tears, no more sorrow. My wife has become my friend. I now listen to her and take her advice. Like a true convert, I want my other friends to learn what I had learned. So I go from house to house, together with my wife and children to dialogue with other households. When they see us, they are shocked and surprised, and want to listen to what had brought about the new image, the change. Invariably they are also touched and the change process goes on and on. Some people do not accept the message of change on the first encounter. As a follow-up strategy, we divide ourselves: husband to husband; wife to wife; children to children. We adopt a one-on-one approach. There is constant interaction at the household level. So far, we have touched the lives of 58 families, but the work goes on and on."

Source: Women for Women International. 2007. "Ending Violence Against Women in Eastern Congo: Preparing Men to Advocate for Women's Rights." p. 22. Washington, D.C.: Women for Women International. http://www.womenforwomen.org/news-women-for-women/files/MensLeadershipFullReport_002.pdf

7 Negotiating Culture: Some Conclusions

The starting point of this report is the universal validity and application of the international human rights framework. Understanding how values, practices and beliefs affect human behaviour is fundamental to the design of effective programmes that help people and nations realize human rights. Nowhere is this understanding more important than in the area of power relations between men and women and their impact on reproductive health and rights. Development practice is firmly located at this nexus of culture, gender relations and human rights. It is from this point that creative and sustainable interventions emerge.

Culture is a source of knowledge, identity and power. Yet, cultures are dynamic, they adapt to changing circumstances, and they themselves contribute to change. The impetus for cultural change may come from external circumstances, but transformations come from within, through processes specific to the culture.

▶ *International development agencies ignore culture – or marginalize it – at their peril. Advancing human rights requires an appreciation of the complexity, fluidity and centrality of culture by intentionally identifying and partnering with local agents of change.*

This partnership is especially valuable in a rapidly changing set of external circumstances, including climate change and economic globalization.

Culturally sensitive approaches, as the means through which culture is successfully negotiated, are about integrating economic, political, social and other dimensions to develop a comprehensive picture of how people function within their social contexts, and why they make the choices they do. In so doing, the report demonstrates the strength of a culturally sensitive approach to realizing gender equality and human rights.

▶ *Approaches based on cultural knowledge provide viability to policymaking – and enable the "cultural politics" required for human rights.*

This report illustrates how deep-rooted cultural beliefs sustain gender inequalities, and how gender-based violence is perpetuated through social and

◀ *A group of older men in Tajikistan. In many cultures, small groups of elders have traditionally made decisions affecting the whole community.*
© Warrick Page/Panos

cultural norms which some women may themselves reinforce and perpetuate. At the same time, advances on gender equality issues have never come without cultural struggles against visible and invisible dimensions of power – that is, a "cultural politics" which involves creating alternatives to dominant cultural meanings.

An approach which interprets a culture by analysing characteristics such as its history, power relationships and dynamics, politics and economics is able to go beyond *how* things are to understand *why* they are the way they are, how they might be changing and what is influencing change. This "cultural politics" is important for effective policymaking; it provides a context, enables strategic partnerships, identifies spaces for intervention and ensures that policies are in line with and support local initiatives.

As the framework of human rights has taken shape, the language and politics of human rights have opened space for cultural changes. People are using the language of rights to make their own claims, because this is the language of resistance to deprivation and oppression which is common to all cultures. Negotiating culture with a focus on human rights effectively questions, delegitimizes and, in the long run, erodes oppression.

Finding out what people believe and think and what makes sense to them, and working with that knowledge, does not require equal acceptance of all values and practices. Cultural fluency offers important insights into harmful cultural beliefs and practices, as well as the positive and empowering aspects which can underpin rights-based practices. This is a necessary and ongoing requirement for consolidating cultural legitimacy to advance human rights.

▶ *Cultural fluency determines how systems of meanings, economic and political opposition or supportive policies develop – and can be developed.*

Population issues at the community, family and individual levels come down to decisions about the number of children to have and when to have them, decisions about health care and health-related behaviour, investments in children (often depending on the gender of the child and anticipated future returns to the family) and the quality of care to provide mother and child. All of these decisions are made within a specific cultural context.

These decisions influence poverty rates and policies in any given country. Maternal mortality rates, for instance, mirror the huge discrepancy between the haves and the have-nots, both within a society and between countries. At the same time, maternal health indicators are used to gauge health systems' performance in terms of access, gender equality and institutional efficiency. These intersectionalities are important dimensions to identify and assess during policy formulation and implementation. Opposition to the provision of information and services – in the area of adolescent reproductive health for instance – even if played out in the political arena, is culturally rooted.

Remittances from migrants are much more than an economic phenomenon – they demonstrate how cultures decipher and translate family and communal responsibilities and obligations to provide security. Similarly, culture plays an important role in determining rejection or acceptance of migrants and policies which host countries adopt in response to migration. Culture is a feature of the dynamics of trafficking, which is damaging to communities of both origin and destination. Cultural fluency entails an awareness of the centrality of culture, of the domain of cultural interactions and of the nature, range and modality of partnerships required to tackle these issues.

▶ *To develop cultural fluency, UNFPA proposes a "culture lens" as a programming tool.*

The culture lens helps to identify the various factors in contesting and changing the practices underpinning gender inequality. It helps UNFPA work with its partners who negotiate with individuals, groups and communities, and build alliances for the realization of human rights through effective programming design.

Culturally informed perspectives appreciate the different dimensions of power, and how power works within cultures. People may value and accept cultural norms without being persuaded to do so; but cultures are also manipulated to sustain power structures and relationships. Visible cultural domination is easier to

▲ Police officers in Haiti. More action is needed to bring women into traditionally male-dominated professions like law enforcement.
© Carina Wint

"real men". Cultural pressures around masculinity, coupled with sexual repression, increase the incidence of rape and other forms of gender-based violence.

Culturally sensitive approaches recognize that social constructions of "gender", "freedom" and "equality" will have different meanings in different cultures; one-size-fits-all interventions can provoke more harm than good. Examples abound from contexts of armed conflict, when men are depicted as aggressors and tyrants and women as passive, ignorant and powerless to change harmful power relations. Such assumptions of vulnerability can blind development assistance providers to the resilience and creativity of people affected by armed conflicts. Such oversimplifications can produce a backlash against development assistance, and play into the hands of those who oppose women's empowerment and gender equality.

▶ *Culturally sensitive approaches call for different analytical and operational frameworks and for introspection among members of the development community.*

Culturally sensitive approaches demand that human realities, fundamentally including cultures, are the basis for policy rather than abstract reasoning, grand theories and generalized assumptions about human preferences and objectives.

Culturally sensitive approaches reject rigid ethnocentrism. They recognize that maternal health and ageing, for example, may have very different meanings in different cultural contexts. They seek to understand those differences and meanings – why and how people (both women and men) think and act the way they do – without assuming that people ought to think and act the way "we" do.

Tackling the ethnocentricities of development institutions can be especially challenging, because reflective practice involves each person confronting his or her own cultural framework. It also requires candid analysis of how organizations and individuals exercise power, and with what effects.

Culturally sensitive approaches avoid wholesale generalizations about people and their cultures. They do not allow for ready-made assumptions about people's intentions, priorities and capacities, but take the time to learn

recognize than the hidden and invisible dimensions of power. Hidden power prevents some issues from even reaching the agenda for discussion. Invisible or internalized power is perhaps the most intractable form. People may accept cultural norms that harm them, because they have negative views of themselves. The different forms of power have differing implications for policy, and culturally sensitive approaches must be attuned to them.

In supporting national efforts towards women's empowerment and gender equality, culturally sensitive approaches go beyond visible power dynamics and seek to understand and respond to how power takes shape in intersecting levels of women's and men's lives (public, private and intimate). These approaches enable an acknowledgement of how cultural pressures around gender can increase men's vulnerability to sexual ill-health by increasing risky behaviour. This, in turn, reduces the likelihood that men will seek help; instead, they may seek multiple partners in their anxiety to prove themselves

about, accommodate and build on people's own efforts. They acknowledge that people within the same cultural contexts can have different values and objectives. They seek the deep local knowledge – the fluency – and relationships that can provide the basis for dialogue and mutual change.

Cultural awareness and engagement will serve very narrow instrumental purposes if the sole objective is to use cultural mechanisms in order to change "others". Culturally sensitive approaches provide a platform for critical reflection on cultures and how they influence development processes. They encourage organizations and individuals concerned with development to confront and change the conventional ways in which they think and work.

This report shows that development practitioners ignore culture at their peril. This is not because culture is everything, but because poverty, poor health, lack of education and conflict also contribute to destroying and undermining culture. There is, therefore, a strong link between cultural fluency, cultural politics and tackling the root causes of distress and denial of human rights.

Cultural fluency is an integral part of a multidimensional approach to development, rather than a distinct and superior method of analysis. Culturally sensitive approaches encourage humility among those who work with communities for the well-being of all their members, without discrimination. They are concerned with building the relationships of recognition, respect and trust which are fundamental for human development.

Notes and Indicators

Notes

CHAPTER 1

1   UNFPA. 1994. "Principles" from the *ICPD Programme of Action* adopted at the International Conference on Population and Development. Cairo: UNFPA.

2   UNFPA. n.d. *State of World Population.* New York: UNFPA.

3   Sen, A. 2004. "How Does Culture Matter?" in *Culture and Public Action,* edited by V. Rao and M. Walton. Stanford: Stanford University Press.

4   See Chapter 2 for an extended discussion.

5   UNESCO. 1997. *Our Creative Diversity: Report of the World Commission on Culture.* Paris: Oxford & IBH Publishing Co. / UNESCO Publishing.

6   UNDP. 2004. *Cultural Liberty in Today's Diverse World.* New York: UNDP.

7   UNFPA. Forthcoming 2008. "Indonesia: Ending violence against women and keeping the faith", in *Programming to Address Violence Against Women: Eight Case Studies.* New York: UNFPA.

8   Ibid.

9   LeBaron, M. 2003. "Culture and Conflict", in *Beyond Intractability,* edited by G. Burgess and H. Burgess. Boulder: Conflict Research Consortium, University of Colorado.

10   UNFPA. 2004. Wole Sovinka, Nigerian Nobel Laureate, quoted in "Quotes on Culture and Culturally Sensitive Approaches". Website: http://www.unfpa.org/culture/quotes.htm, accessed 15 June 2008.

11   UNFPA. 2004. Culture Matters: Working with Communities and *Faith-based Organizations—Case Studies from Country Programmes.* New York: UNFPA.

12   Geertz, C. 1973. *The Interpretation of Cultures: Selected Essays.* New York: Basic Books.

13   UNFPA. 2004. "Quotes on Culture and Culturally Sensitive Approaches". Website: http://www.unfpa.org/culture/quotes.htm, accessed 15 June 2008.

14   Ross, M.H. 1997. "Culture and Identity in Comparative Political Analysis" in *Comparative Politics: rationality, culture and structure,* edited by M. Lichbach and A. Zuckerman. Cambridge: Cambridge University Press.

15   Schalkwyk J. 2000. "Culture, Gender Equality and Development Cooperation". Unpublished paper prepared for Canadian International Development Agency.

16   Bourdieu, P. 1980. *The Logic of Practice.* Stanford: Stanford University Press.

17   Ross, M.H. 1997. Op. cit.

18   Chabal, P. and J. Daloz. 1988. *Culture Troubles: Politics and the Interpretation of Meaning.* London: Hurst and Company.

19   Ibid.

20   UNESCO. 2001. *Universal Declaration on Cultural Diversity.* Paris: UNESCO.

21   Sen, A. 2004. Op. cit.

22   Bourdieu, P. 1980. Op.cit.

23   UNFPA. 2004. Pastor Pax Tan Chiow Lian, quoted in "Quotes on Culture and Culturally Sensitive Approaches". Website: http://www.unfpa.org/culture/quotes.htm, accessed 15 June 2008.

24   Said, E. 2003. *Orientalism: Western Conceptions of the Orient,* London: Penguin Books.

25   Mohanty, C. 2003. *Feminism Without Borders: Decolonizing Theory, Practising Solidarity.* Durham: Duke University Press.

26   Marshall, K. 2005. "Religious Faith and Development: Rethinking Development Debates". Paper presented at Religious NGOs and International Development Conference, Oslo, Norway, 7 April 2005. Website: http://www.vanderbilt.edu/csrc/PDFs%20and%20Jpgs/marshall-debates.pdf, accessed 15 June 2008.

27   Knutsson, K.E. 2005. "Without Culture, No Sustainable Development: Some reflections on the topic". Unpublished paper presented at the seminar "Research Collaboration in the Fields of Culture and Sustainable Development", held at Stjernsund, Sweden in September 2000.

28   United Nations. 1986. *Declaration on the Right to Development* (A/RES/41/128). New York: United Nations General Assembly.

29   Harragin, S. 2004. "Relief and an Understanding of Local Knowledge: The Case of Southern Sudan", in *Culture and Public Action,* edited by V. Rao and M. Walton. Stanford: Stanford University Press.

30   Njoh, A. 2006. *Tradition, Culture and Development in Africa.* Burlington: Ashgate Publishing Company.

31   Chabal, P. and J. Daloz. 1988. *Culture Troubles: Politics and the Interpretation of Meaning.* London: Hurst and Company.

32   Geertz, C. 1983. *Local Knowledge: further essays in interpretive anthropology.* London: Perseus Books.

33   Murray, S. 2001. *Changing Culture, Changing Rights.* Oxford: Oxford University Press.

34   An-Na'im, A. 1990. "Problems of Universal Cultural Legitimacy for Human Rights", in *Human Rights in Africa: Cross-Cultural Perspectives,* edited by A. An-Na'im and F. M. Deng. Washington DC: Brookings Institution Press.

CHAPTER 2

1   An-Na'im, A. 1990. *Toward an Islamic Reformation: Civil Liberties, Human Rights and International Law.* Syracuse: Syracuse University Press.

2   United Nations. 1945. *Charter of the United Nations.* San Francisco: United Nations.

3   United Nations. 1948. *Universal Declaration of Human Rights.* San Francisco: United Nations.

4   Ibid.

5   Ibid.

6   Nyamu-Musembi, C. 2005. "Toward an Actor-Oriented Perspective on Human Rights", in *Meanings and Expressions of Citizenship: Perspectives from the North and South,* edited by N. Kabeer. London: Zed Books.

7   Chanock, M. 2002. "Human Rights and Cultural Branding: Who Speaks and How", in *Cultural Transformation and Human Rights in Africa,* edited by A. An-na'im. London: Zed Books.

8   American Anthropological Association. 1947. "Statement on Human Rights", *American Anthropologist,* 49: 539.

9   Murray, S. 2001. *Changing Culture, Changing Rights.* Oxford: Oxford University Press.

10   Nyamu-Musembi, C. 2005. "Toward an Actor-Oriented Perspective on Human Rights", in *Meanings and Expressions of Citizenship: Perspectives from the North and South,* edited by N. Kabeer. London: Zed Books.

11   UNFPA. 2003. *Addressing Violence against Women: Piloting and Programming.* New York: UNFPA.

12   UNFPA. 2008. Lao Tsu, quoted in *Integrating Human Rights, Culture and Gender In Programming Trainer's Guide,* Culture Training Workshop, Brasilia, Brazil, June 2008.

13   Sen, A. 2004. "How Does Culture Matter?" in *Culture and Public Action,* edited by V. Rao and M. Walton. Stanford: Stanford University Press.

14   An Na'im, 1990. "Human Rights in the Muslim World: Socio-Political Conditions and Scriptural Imperatives" in *Harvard Human Rights Journal.* Volume 3, Spring: 20.

15   An Na'im, A. 1992. "Toward a Cross-Cultural Approach to Defining International Standards of Human Rights", in *Human Rights in Cross-Cultural Perspective,* edited by A. An Na'im. Philadelphia: University of Philadelphia Press.

16   UNFPA. 2008. *Integrating Human Rights, Culture and Gender In Programming Trainer's Guide,* Culture Training Workshop, Brasilia, Brazil, June 2008.

17   An Na'im, 1990. Op. Cit.

18   An Na'im, A. 1992. Op.cit.

19   Thoraya Ahmed Obaid, Executive Director UNFPA.

20   UNFPA. 2004. *Culture Matters: Working with Communities and Faith-based Organizations—Case Studies from Country Programmes.* New York: UNFPA.

21   Nyamu-Musembi, C. 2002. "Are Local Norms and Practices Fences or Pathways? The Example of Women's Property Rights", in

Cultural Transformation and Human Rights in Africa, edited by A. An Na'im. London: Zed Books.

22 Clark, C. and M. Reilly. *Rights-Based Approaches and Beyond: Challenges of Linking Rights and Participation*. Sussex: Institute of Development Studies.

23 UNFPA. 2008. *Integrating Human Rights, Culture and Gender In Programming Trainer's Guide*, Culture Training Workshop, Brasilia, Brazil, June 2008.

24 United Nations. 2007. *Report of the Special Rapporteur on violence against women, its causes and consequences – Intersections between culture and violence against women* (A/HRC/4/34). New York: United Nations.

CHAPTER 3

1 Professor Cecilia Sardenberg contributed some of the text for this chapter and also wrote a background paper.

2 UNFPA. 2008. Lao Tsu, quoted in *Integrating Human Rights, Culture and Gender In Programming Trainer's Guide*, Culture Training Workshop, Brasilia, Brazil, June 2008.

3 United Nations. 1995. *Beijing Platform of Action*. New York: United Nations, Department of Economic and Social Affairs, Division for the Advancement of Women.

4 UNFPA. 2008. *Gender Equality: An End in Itself and a Cornerstone of Development*. Website: http://www.unfpa.org/gender/index.htm, accessed 15 June 2008.

5 United Nations. 1995. *Beijing Platform of Action*, op cit.

6 United Nations. 1995. *Beijing Platform of Action*, op. cit. Articles 38-40.

7 United Nations. 2000. "Women 2000: Gender Equality, Development and Peace for the Twenty-first Century". United Nations General Assembly Special Session, New York, 5-9 June 2000.

8 United Nations. 2000. *Millennium Declaration* (A.55.2). New York: United Nations.

9 UNFPA. 2005. *Cultural Programming: Reproductive Health Challenges and Strategies in East*

and South-East Asia. New York: UNFPA

10 Hawthorne, S. M. 2006. *Origins, Genealogies, and the Politics of Identity: Towards a Feminist Philosophy Of Myth*. London: School of Oriental and Asian Studies.

11 Spindel, Cheywa, Elisa Levy and Melissa Connor. 2000. *With an End in Sight: Strategies from the UNIFEM Trust Fund to Eliminate Violence Against Women*. New York: UNIFEM.

12 IMF. 2000. *Poverty Reduction Strategy Paper—Uganda's Poverty Eradication Action Plan Summary and Main Objectives*. Kampala: Ministry of Finance, Planning and Economic Development.

13 Yates J. and J. Moncrieffe. 2002. *Synthesis of Uganda's Participatory Poverty Assessment Cycle 1 Findings*. London: Earthscan.

14 Bachrach, P. and M. Baratz. 1962. "Two Faces of Power", in *The American Political Science Review* 56(4): 947-952.

15 Ibid.

16 Veneklasen, L. with V. Miller. 2002. *A New Weave of Power, People and Politics*. Warwickshire: Practical Action Publishing.

17 Chanock, M. 2002. "Human Rights and Cultural Branding: Who Speaks and How?" in *Cultural Transformation and Human Rights in Africa*, edited by A. An-na'im. London: Zed Books.

18 Chanock, M. 2002. Op. cit.

19 UNFPA. 2005. Op. cit.

20 Sardenberg C. 2007. "Negotiating Cultures: Promoting Gender Equality and Empowering Women". Background Paper for the *State of World Population Report 2008*, New York: UNFPA.

21 In accordance with General Assembly Resolution A/RES/62/208, UNFPA's "operational activities are carried out for the benefit of programme countries, at the request of those countries and in accordance with their own policies and priorities for development".

22 UNFPA. 1994. *ICPD Programme of Action*, para 1.15. New York: UNFPA.

23 Veneklasen, L. with V. Miller. 2002. Op. cit.

24 UNFPA. 2008. *Integrating Human Rights, Culture and Gender In Programming Trainer's Guide*, Culture Training Workshop, Brasilia, Brazil, June 2008.

25 Veneklasen, L. with V. Miller. 2002. Op. cit.

26 Banda and Chinkin, 2004. *Gender, Minorities and Indigenous Peoples*, London: MRG.

27 Ibid.

28 Ibid.

29 UNFPA. 2008. Op. cit.

30 Rao, V. and M. Walton, 2006. *Culture and Public Action*. Stanford: Stanford University Press.

31 Lavrin, A. 1998. "International Feminisms: Latin American Alternatives", in *Gender & History*, Vol. 10(3): 525.

32 Ibid.

33 Nyamu-Musembi, C. 2005. "An Actor Oriented Approach to Rights in Development", in *Developing Rights*? IDS Bulletin , Volume 36, Number 1. Sussex: Institute of Development Studies.

34 Women, Faith and Development Alliance. "Mission". Website: http://www.wfd-alliance.org/AUmission.htm, accessed 15 June 2008.

35 The African Women's Development and Communication Network (FEMNET). 2008. Website: http://www.femnet.or.ke/subsubsection.asp?ID=8, accessed 15 June 2008.

36 UNFPA. 2008. Op. cit.

37 IDS. 2008. *Report on the Politicising Masculinities Symposium*. Sussex: Institute for Development Studies. Website: http://64.233.169.104/search?q=cache:v_XjaZ2-FHEJ:www.siyanda.org/docs/esplen_greig_masculinities.pdf+IDS+2008,+Report+on+the+Politicising+Masculinities+Symposium&hl=en&ct=clnk&cd=4&gl=us, accessed 15 June 2008.

38 Ibid.

39 Ibid.

40 UNFPA. 2006. "Ending Violence Against Women". Website: http://www.unfpa.org/

endingviolence/, accessed 15 June 2008.

41 UNFPA. 2006. "Kindling Hope in Northern Ethiopia by Keeping Adolescent Girls in School", in *UNFPA Feature*. Website: http://www.unfpa.org/news/news.cfm?ID=947&Language=1, accessed 15 June 2008.

CHAPTER 4

1 UNFPA. 1994. *ICPD Programme of Action*, adopted at the International Conference on Population and Development. New York: UNFPA.

2 United Nations. 2006. *Report of the Secretary-General: In-depth Study on all Forms of Violence Against Women*. New York: United Nations.

3 Men for Gender Equality Now—a Kenyan network of men working to end gender based violence. 2008. Website: http://www.changemakers.net/en-us/node/313, accessed 19 June 2008.

4 International Development Research Center. 2008. *Addressing Violence Against Palestinian Women*. IDRC Bulletin. Website: http://www.idrc.ca/en/ev-5311-201-1-DO_TOPIC.html, accessed 19 June 2008.

5 Inhorn, M. and F. Van Balen. 2002. *Infertility around the Globe: New Thinking on Childlessness, Gender, and Reproductive Technologies*. Berkeley: University of California Press.

6 Visaria, L., 2007. "Deficit of Girls in India: Can It be Attributed to Female Selective Abortion?" in *Sex Selective Abortion in India*, edited by T. Patel. Delhi: Sage Publications.

7 Inhorn, M. and F. Van Balen. 2002. *Infertility around the Globe: New Thinking on Childlessness, Gender, and Reproductive Technologies*. Berkeley: University of California Press.

8 Ibid.

9 UNFPA and UNICEF. "The Government of Guinea Bissau, in Partnership with UNICEF and UNFPA, Launches a Joint Programme for the Abandonment of Female Genital Mutilation Through Tostan Community-Led

Strategy." Press Release, 9 June 2008, New York.

10 Dudgeon, M. and M. Inhorn. 2004. "Men's influences on women's reproductive health: medical anthropological perspectives", in *Social Science and Medicine.* (59):1379-1395.

11 UNFPA. 2006. "Lessons from the Field—Cambodia". Website: http://www.unfpa.org/culture/case_studies/cambodia.htm, accessed 15 June 2008.

12 UNFPA. 2006. "Zimbabwe: Indigenous Christian Churches Make an About Turn on HIV Prevention", in *New Feature.* Website: http://www.unfpa.org/news/news.cfm?ID=786, accessed 15 June 2008.

13 UNFPA. 2008. *Preventionls for Life, HIV/AIDS: Dispatches from the Field.* New York: UNFPA.

14 UNDP, Population Association, and UNFPA. 2007. *The Dynamics of Honour Killings in Turkey: Prospects for Action.* New York: UNFPA and UNDP.

15 United Nations. 2006. *Report of the Secretary-General: In-depth Study on all Forms of Violence Against Women.* New York: United Nations.

16 Ibid.

17 UNFPA. 2006. "Maternal Morbidity: Surviving Childbirth, but Enduring Chronic Ill-Health." *Maternal Health Fact Sheet.* Website: http://www.unfpa.org/mothers/morbidity.htm, accessed 15 June 2008.

18 UNFPA. 2008. "Good Neighbours: UNFPA Trains Nigerian Men and Women to Bring Better Reproductive Health to their Communities", in *UNFPA Feature Story.* Website: http://www.unfpa.org/news/news.cfm?ID=1087, accessed 19 June 2008.

19 UNFPA. 2008. "Campaign to End Fistula—Sudan". Website: http://www.endfistula.org/sudan.htm, accessed 15 June 2008.

20 UNFPA. 2008. "Campaign to End Fistula". Website: http://www.endfistula.org, accessed 15 June 2008.

21 Ibid.

22 United Nations. 1995. *Beijing Platform of Action.* New York: United Nations, Department of Economic and Social Affairs,

Division for the Advancement of Women.

23 United Nations. 2001. *Declaration of Commitment on HIV/AIDS.* (A/26/2). New York: United Nations.

24 Dudgeon, M. and M. Inhorn. 2004. Op. cit.

25 Alan Guttmacher Institute. 2003. *In Their Own Right: Addressing the Sexual and Reproductive Health Needs of Men Worldwide.* New York: AGI.

26 Weiss, E. and G.R. Gupta. 1998. *Bridging the Gap: Addressing Gender and Sexuality in HIV Prevention.* Washington, DC: International Center for Research on Women.

27 Orubuloye, I.O. and J.C. Caldwell. 1993. "African Women's Control over their Sexuality in an Era of AIDS: A study of the Yoruba of Nigeria", in *Social Science & Medicine* (37):859-872.

28 Mane, P. and P. Aggleton. 2001. "Gender and HIV/AIDS: What Do Men Have to Do with It?" *Current Sociology* 49(6): 23-37.

29 Rivers, K. and P. Aggleton. 2001. *Men and the HIV Epidemic.* New York, United Nations Development Programme.

30 Weiss, E. and G.R. Gupta. 1998. Op. cit.

31 Rivers, K. and P. Aggleton. 2001. Op. cit.

32 Magongo, B., S. Magwaza, V. Mathambo and N. Makhanya. 2002. "National Report on the Assessment of the Public Sector's Voluntary Counselling and Testing Programme". Durban: Health Systems Trust.

33 Weiss, E. and G.R. Gupta. 1998. *Bridging the Gap: Addressing Gender and Sexuality in HIV Prevention.* Washington, DC: International Center for Research on Women.

34 Hudspeth, J., W.D.F. Venter, A. Van Rie, J. Wing and C. Feldman. 2004. "Access to and early outcomes of a public South African antiretroviral clinic", in *The Southern African Journal of Epidemiology and Infection* 19(2): 48-51.

35 Nachega, J., M. Hislop, D. Dowdy, M. Lo, S. Omer, L. Regensberg, R. Chaisson and G. Maartens. 2006. "Adherence to Highly Active Antiretroviral Therapy Assessed

by Pharmacy Claims Predicts Survival in HIV-Infected South African Adults", in *Journal of Acquired Immune Deficiency Syndromes* 43(1): 78-84.

36 Population Council. 2004. "Involving Young Men in HIV Prevention Programs: Operations research on gender-based approaches in Brazil, Tanzania, and India", in *Horizons.* New York: Population Council.

37 Rivers, K. and P. Aggleton. 2001. Op. cit.

38 Population Council. 2004. Op. cit.

CHAPTER 5

1 Sen A. 1993. "Capability and well-being", in *The Quality of Life. A study prepared for World Institute for Development Economics Research,* edited by M. Nussbaum and A. Sen. Oxford: Oxford University Press.

2 UNDP. 2004. *Human Development Report: Cultural liberty in today's diverse world.* New York: United Nations Development Programme.

3 World Bank. 2007. *Socio-economic differences in health, nutrition and population within developing countries, An Overview, Country reports on HNP and poverty.* Washington D.C.: World Bank.

4 Ibid.

5 Merrick, T. 2002. "Population and poverty: New views on an old controversy", in *International Family Planning Perspectives.* 28(1).

6 Abbasi-Shavazi, M. 2002. "Recent changes and the future of fertility in Iran". Report presented at the United Nations Expert Group meeting on Completing the Fertility Transition (ESA/P/WP.172). New York: United Nations.

7 Cleland, J. 1994. *The determinants of reproductive change in Bangladesh: Success in a challenging environment.* Washington D.C.: World Bank.

8 Unnithan, M. 2004. "Conception technologies, local healers and negotiations around childbearing in Rajasthan". Chapter 5 in *Reproductive Agency, Medicine and the State: Cultural Transformations in Childbearing, Fertility, Reproduction and Sexuality.* New York: Berghahn Books.

9 UNFPA. 2006. "Facts About Safe Motherhood". Website:

http://www.unfpa.org/mothers/facts.htm, accessed 15 June 2008.

10 WHO. 2004. *Making pregnancy safer: The critical role of the skilled attendant—A joint statement by WHO, ICM and FIGO.* Geneva: World Health Organization.

11 WHO. 2008. "Proportion of births attended by a skilled health worker—2008 updates". Fact Sheet, Department of Reproductive Health and Research Fact Sheet. Geneva: World Health Organization.

12 Wilder, J. 2008. "Ethiopia's Health Extension Program: Pathfinder International's support 2003-2007". Addis Ababa: Pathfinder International.

13 UNAIDS. 2007. 2007 *AIDS epidemic update—Joint report of UNAIDS and WHO.* Geneva: Joint United Nations Programme on HIV/AIDS.

14 United Nations. 2006. *International migration and development, Report of the Secretary General (A/60/871).* New York: United Nations.

15 World Bank. 2008. *Global Economic Prospects 2006. Technology Diffusion in the Developing World.* Washington, D.C.: World Bank.

16 Fajnzylber, P. and H. Lopez. 2006. *Close to Home: The Development Impact of Remittances in Latin America.* Washington D.C.: World Bank.

17 UNFPA. 2006. *State of World Population: A Passage to Hope—Women and International Migration.* New York: UNFPA.

18 Unnithan, M. 2004. Op. cit.

19 Ibid.

CHAPTER 6

1 Stockholm International Peace Research Institute. 2008. *SIPRI Yearbook 2008: Armaments, Disarmament and International Security.* Oxford: Oxford University Press.

2 El Jack, A. 2003. *Gender and Armed Conflict.* Sussex: Institute of Development Studies.

3 Women for Women International. 2007. "Ending Violence Against Women in Eastern Congo: Preparing Men to Advocate for Women's Rights", in Women for Women *Quarterly Report,* Winter 2007. Website: http://www.womenforwomen.org/

news-women-for-women/files/
MensLeadershipFullReport_002.pdf,
accessed 15 June 2008.

4   Byrne, B. 1996. "Towards a gen-
    dered understanding of conflict",
    in Institute for Development
    Studies *Bulletin* 27(3) 31–40.
    Sussex: IDS.

5   The Advocates for Human Rights.
    2008. "Sexual Assault During
    Armed Conflict". Stop Violence
    Against Women website:
    www.stopvaw.org/Sexual_Assault
    _During_Armed_Conflict.html,
    accessed 15 June 2008.

6   Dolan, C. 2002. "Collapsing
    Masculinities and Weak States",
    in F. Cleaver, ed., *Masculinities
    Matter*. London: Zed Books.

7   Byrne, B. 1996. Op. cit.

8   UNICEF, UNFPA, UNIFEM. 2008.
    *A Rapid Assessment of Gender-
    based Violence During the
    Post-Election Violence in Kenya*.
    New York: UNICEF, UNFPA,
    UNIFEM.

9   Dolan, C. 2002. Op. cit.

10 United Nations. 2000. "United
    Nations Security Council
    Resolution 1325 on Women,
    Peace and Security."
    (S/RES/1325). New York:
    United Nations.

11 United Nations. 2000. *Windhoek
    Declaration and the Namibia Plan of
    Action on Mainstreaming a Gender
    Perspective in Multidimensional
    Peace Support Operations*.
    Adopted in Windhoek, Namibia
    on 31 May 2000. Website:
    www.un.org/womenwatch/osagi/
    wps/windhoek_declaration.pdf,
    accessed 15 June 2008.

12 El Jack, A. 2003. *Gender and
    Armed Conflict*. Sussex: Institute
    of Development Studies.

13 UNFPA. 2006. *Women are the
    Fabric: Reproductive Health for
    Communities in Crisis*. New York:
    UNFPA.

14 Byrne, B. 1996. Op. cit.

15 El Jack, A. 2003. Op. cit.

16 Ibid.

17 Ibid.

18 Ibid.

19 Ibid.

20 UNICEF, UNFPA, UNIFEM. 2008.
    Op. cit.

21 Ibid.

22 Best, M. and P. Hussey. 2005. *A
    Culture of Peace: Women, Faith and
    Reconciliation*. London: Catholic
    Institute for International
    Relations.

23 Byrne, B. 1996. Op. cit.

24 Women's Commission for
    Refugee Women and Children.
    2008. *Disabilities among Refugees
    and Conflict Affected Populations*.
    New York: Women's Commission.

25 Women for Women International.
    2007. Op. cit.

26 Magcalen-Fernandez, E. 2006.
    *Conflict, State Fragility and
    Women's Reproductive Health:
    The Case of Basilan, Philippines*.
    Washington DC: USAID.

27 Women's Commission for
    Refugee Women and Children.
    2008. *Disabilities among Refugees
    and Conflict Affected Populations*.
    New York: Women's Commission.

28 The Pew Forum on Religion and
    Public Life. 2008. "Ugandan
    Religious Leaders Set Aside
    Rivalries in Pursuit of Peace".
    News Update. Washington DC:
    Pew Forum. Website: http://
    pewforum.org/news/display.php?
    NewsID=14725, accessed 20
    June 2008.

29 UNFPA. 2006. Op. cit.

30 Catholic Relief Services. 2008.
    Newsletter. Website: http://crs.org/
    peacebuilding/dialogue.cfm,
    accessed 19 June 2008.

31 Islamic Relief Worldwide. 2008.
    Website: http://www.islamic-
    relief.com/, accessed 19 June
    2008.

32 UNFPA. 2008. "Protecting
    Reproductive Health in Times
    of Crisis". *UNFPA Fact Sheet*.
    Website: http://www.unfpa.org/
    emergencies/rh.htm, accessed
    15 June 2008.

33 Refugee Studies Centre. 1999.
    "Culture in Exile", in *Forced
    Migration Review*. Oslo: Refugee
    Studies Centre. Website:
    http://www.fmreview.org/
    FMRpdfs/FMR06/fmr6full.pdf,
    accessed 15 June 2008.

34 Women for Women International.
    2006. "Psychosocial Challenges
    and Interventions for Women
    Affected by Conflict", in *Critical
    Half: Bi-Annual Journal of Women
    for Women International*. 4(1):
    Summer 2006. Website:
    http://www.womenforwomen.org
    /documents/CH5.pdf, accessed
    15 June 2008.

35 Ibid.

36 International Crisis Group. 2006.
    "Beyond Victimhood: Women's
    Peacebuilding in Sudan, Congo
    and Uganda." *Africa Report No.
    112*, 28 June 2006. Website:
    http://www.crisisgroup.org/
    home/index.cfm?id=4185&f=1,
    accessed 15 June 2008.

37 Refugee Studies Centre. 1999.
    Op. cit.

38 Ibid.

39 Women for Women International.
    2006. Op. cit.

40 Ibid.

Monitoring ICPD Goals – Selected Indicators

	Indicators of Mortality			Indicators of Education				Reproductive Health Indicators			
	Infant mortality Total per 1,000 live births	Life expectancy M/F	Maternal mortality ratio	Primary enrolment (gross) M/F	Proportion reaching grade 5 M/F	Secondary enrolment (gross) M/F	% Illiterate (>15 years) M/F	Births per 1,000 women aged 15-19	Contraceptive Prevalence Any method	Modern methods	HIV prevalence rate (%) (15-49) M/F
World Total	49	65.1 / 69.6						53	62	55	
More developed regions (*)	7	73.0 / 80.2						23	68	57	
Less developed regions (+)	54	63.8 / 67.4						57	61	55	
Least developed countries (‡)	87	53.6 / 56.0						116	30	23	
AFRICA (1)	86	51.9 / 53.9						104	27	22	
EASTERN AFRICA	81	50.2 / 52.0						107	25	20	
Burundi	99	48.3 / 51.1	1,100	108 / 98	84 / 92	16 / 12	33 / 48	55	20	9	1.6 / 2.4
Eritrea	55	55.8 / 60.4	450	69 / 56	77 / 70	39 / 23		72	8	5	1.0 / 1.5
Ethiopia	86	51.8 / 54.4	720	97 / 85	64 / 65	37 / 24	50 / 77	94	15	14	1.6 / 2.4
Kenya	64	53.1 / 55.3	560	107 / 104	81 / 85	52 / 49	22 / 30	104	39	32	
Madagascar	65	57.8 / 61.5	510	142 / 137	35 / 37	24 / 23	23 / 35	133	27	17	0.2 / 0.1
Malawi	88	48.1 / 48.4	1,100	117 / 121	44 / 44	32 / 27	25 / 46	135	42	39	10.3 / 13.5
Mauritius (2)	14	69.6 / 76.3	15	102 / 102	98 / 100	89 / 88	12 / 19	41	76	41	2.4 / 1.0
Mozambique	95	41.9 / 42.5	520	113 / 97	60 / 55	18 / 13	45 / 75	149	17	12	10.1 / 14.9
Rwanda	112	44.9 / 48.2	1,300	138 / 142	43 / 49	14 / 13	29 / 40	40	17	10	2.3 / 3.2
Somalia	115	47.1 / 49.6	1,400					66	15	1	0.8 / 0.3
Uganda	76	51.0 / 52.5	550	116 / 117	49 / 49	20 / 16	22 / 41	152	24	18	4.3 / 6.6
United Republic of Tanzania	71	51.5 / 53.7	950	113 / 111	85 / 89	7 / 6	22 / 38	121	26	20	5.0 / 7.6
Zambia	92	42.2 / 42.5	830	118 / 116	92 / 87	33 / 27	24 / 40	125	34	23	12.4 / 18.0
Zimbabwe	57	44.2 / 42.8	880	102 / 101	68 / 71	39 / 14	7 / 14	59	60	58	12.2 / 18.7
MIDDLE AFRICA (3)	111	46.0 / 48.4						178	20	6	
Angola	131	41.4 / 44.4	1,400	69 / 59		19 / 16	17 / 46	138	6	5	1.7 / 2.5
Cameroon	87	50.1 / 51.0	1,000	117 / 98	64 / 64	27 / 21	23 / 40	118	26	13	3.9 / 6.3
Central African Republic	96	43.4 / 46.1	980	72 / 49	53 / 45		35 / 66	115	19	9	4.6 / 8.0
Chad	119	49.4 / 51.2	1,500	90 / 61	34 / 32	23 / 8	59 / 87	164	3	2	2.8 / 4.2
Congo, Democratic Republic of the (4)	113	45.3 / 47.9	1,100	68 / 54		28 / 16	19 / 46	222	21	6	2.8 / 4.2
Congo, Republic of	70	54.1 / 56.6	740	113 / 102	65 / 67	47 / 39	10 / 21	115	44	13	2.8 / 4.2
Gabon	53	56.7 / 57.3	520	153 / 152	68 / 71	53 / 46	12 / 21	82	33	12	4.8 / 7.1
NORTHERN AFRICA (5)	38	66.9 / 70.9						31	51	46	
Algeria	30	71.0 / 73.9	180	114 / 106	95 / 96	80 / 86	20 / 40	7	61	52	0.1 / 0.1
Egypt	29	69.3 / 73.8	130	108 / 102	96 / 97	91 / 85	33 / 56	39	59	57	<0.1 /< 0.1
Libyan Arab Jamahiriya	18	71.8 / 77.0	97	113 / 108		86 / 101	7 / 24	3	45	26	
Morocco	30	69.1 / 73.6	240	112 / 100	82 / 79	53 / 45	34 / 60	19	63	55	0.2 / 0.1
Sudan	64	57.2 / 60.2	450	71 / 61	78 / 79	35 / 33	29 / 48	57	8	6	1.1 / 1.7
Tunisia	19	72.0 / 76.2	100	110 / 107	97 / 97	81 / 89	17 / 35	7	63	53	0.1 / <0.1
SOUTHERN AFRICA	46	48.5 / 49.1						61	58	58	
Botswana	46	50.3 / 50.3	380	108 / 106	80 / 85	75 / 78	20 / 18	52	44	42	18.9 / 28.9
Lesotho	64	42.9 / 42.2	960	115 / 114	68 / 80	33 / 42	26 / 10	74	37	35	19.4 / 27.1
Namibia	41	52.2 / 52.6	210	107 / 107	84 / 90	53 / 61	13 / 16	59	44	43	12.2 / 18.6
South Africa	45	48.8 / 49.6	400	108 / 103	82 / 83	92 / 98	16 / 19	61	60	60	14.5 / 21.8
Swaziland	70	39.6 / 39.1	390	110 / 102	81 / 87	47 / 47	19 / 22	33	46	46	20.2 / 32.1
WESTERN AFRICA (6)	105	49.7 / 51.2						124	13	8	
Benin	97	55.8 / 58.0	840	105 / 87	72 / 71	41 / 23	52 / 77	120	17	6	0.9 / 1.6
Burkina Faso	104	50.8 / 53.9	700	66 / 54	72 / 74	17 / 12	71 / 85	126	14	9	1.5 / 1.7
Côte d'Ivoire	116	47.6 / 49.3	810	79 / 62	88 / 87	32 / 18	39 / 61	107	13	8	3.1 / 4.7
Gambia	74	58.8 / 60.5	690	71 / 77		47 / 43		104	18	13	0.7 / 1.0

	Indicators of Mortality			Indicators of Education				Reproductive Health Indicators			
	Infant mortality Total per 1,000 live births	Life expectancy M/F	Maternal mortality ratio	Primary enrolment (gross) M/F	Proportion reaching grade 5 M/F	Secondary enrolment (gross) M/F	% Illiterate (>15 years) M/F	Births per 1,000 women aged 15-19	Contraceptive Prevalence Any method	Contraceptive Prevalence Modern methods	HIV prevalence rate (%) (15-49) M/F
Ghana	56	59.7 / 60.6	560	98 / 97	62 / 65	52 / 46	34 / 50	55	17	14	1.6 / 2.3
Guinea	102	54.7 / 57.9	910	96 / 81	83 / 78	45 / 24	57 / 82	149	9	6	1.3 / 2.0
Guinea-Bissau	112	45.1 / 48.1	1,100	84 / 56		23 / 13	29 / 52	189	10	6	1.5 / 2.2
Liberia	131	45.0 / 46.7	1,200	96 / 87		37 / 27	42 / 54	219	6	6	1.4 / 2.1
Mali	128	52.3 / 56.7	970	90 / 71	83 / 80	35 / 21	67 / 84	179	8	7	1.2 / 1.8
Mauritania	63	62.5 / 66.2	820	99 / 104	59 / 56	27 / 23	40 / 57	85	8	5	1.2 / 0.5
Niger	109	58.0 / 56.2	1,800	58 / 43	58 / 54	14 / 9	91 / 91	196	11	5	1.1 / 0.5
Nigeria	109	46.5 / 47.4	1,100	105 / 87	71 / 75	36 / 29	22 / 40	126	13	8	2.5 / 3.8
Senegal	65	61.2 / 65.3	980	81 / 79	65 / 65	27 / 21	49 / 71	87	12	10	0.8 / 1.2
Sierra Leone	160	41.1 / 44.3	2,100	155 / 139		38 / 26	53 / 76	160	5	4	1.4 / 2.0
Togo	88	56.8 / 60.3	510	110 / 95	79 / 70	54 / 27	31 / 61	89	17	11	2.6 / 3.9
ASIA	**43**	**67.3 / 71.2**						**40**	**66**	**60**	
EASTERN ASIA (7)	**22**	**72.2 / 76.4**						**8**	**85**	**83**	
China	23	71.4 / 74.9	45	112 / 111		75 / 76	5 / 13	8	87	86	0.1 / 0.1
Democratic People's Republic of Korea	48	65.1 / 69.3	370					1	69	58	1.1 / 1.6
Hong Kong SAR, China (8)	4	79.5 / 85.2		97 / 92	99 / 100	85 / 85		5	84	76	
Japan	3	79.1 / 86.2	6[9]	100 / 100		101 / 102		3	54	44	<0.1 /<0.1
Mongolia	39	64.0 / 70.1	46	99 / 102		84 / 95	2 / 2	45	66	61	0.1 / <0.1
Republic of Korea	4	75.1 / 82.3	14	107 / 103	99 / 100	100 / 95		4	81	67	0.1 / <0.1
SOUTH-EASTERN ASIA	**27**	**68.2 / 73.0**						**34**	**58**	**51**	
Cambodia	62	57.6 / 62.1	540	127 / 118	61 / 64	43 / 34	15 / 36	42	40	27	1.2 / 0.5
Indonesia	26	68.8 / 72.8	420	116 / 112	83 / 86	64 / 64	6 / 13	40	58	58	0.3 / 0.1
Lao People's Democratic Republic	50	63.2 / 66.0	660	123 / 109	62 / 62	49 / 38	23 / 39	72	32	29	0.3 / 0.1
Malaysia	9	72.1 / 76.8	62	101 / 100	99 / 100	66 / 72	8 / 15	13	55	30	0.8 / 0.3
Myanmar	65	59.3 / 65.4	380	114 / 115	71 / 72	49 / 49	6 / 14	16	37	33	0.8 / 0.6
Philippines	23	69.6 / 74.1	230	110 / 109	70 / 78	79 / 88	8 / 6	47	51	36	<0.1 / <0.1
Singapore	3	78.1 / 82.0	14				3 / 11	5	62	53	0.2 / 0.1
Thailand	10	66.5 / 75.0	110	108 / 108		75 / 82	5 / 9	42	72	70	1.7 / 1.2
Timor-Leste, Democratic Republic of	65	60.2 / 62.0	380	103 / 95		53 / 54		54	10	9	<0.1 / <0.1
Viet Nam	19	72.5 / 76.4	150	92 / 88	87 / 87	76 / 75	6 / 13	18	76	60	0.8 / 0.3
SOUTH CENTRAL ASIA	**57**	**63.2 / 66.3**						**63**	**53**	**45**	
Afghanistan	156	44.0 / 43.9	1,800	126 / 75		28 / 9	57 / 87	113	19	16	<0.1 / <0.1
Bangladesh	51	63.4 / 65.3	570	101 / 105	63 / 67	43 / 45	46 / 59	125	58	47	<0.1 / <0.1
Bhutan	44	64.3 / 67.8	440	103 / 101	91 / 95	51 / 46		37	31	31	0.1 / < 0.1
India	54	63.3 / 66.6	450	116 / 113	73 / 73	59 / 49	27 / 52	62	56	49	0.4 / 0.3
Iran (Islamic Republic of)	30	69.5 / 72.8	140	104 / 132	88 / 88	83 / 78	16 / 30	20	74	56	0.3 / 0.1
Nepal	53	63.4 / 64.5	830	129 / 123	75 / 83	46 / 41	37 / 65	115	48	44	0.7 / 0.3
Pakistan	67	65.4 / 65.9	320	94 / 74	68 / 72	34 / 26	45 / 71	36	26	18	0.1 / 0.1
Sri Lanka	11	68.8 / 76.3	58	108 / 108		86 / 88	8 / 11	25	70	50	<0.1 / <0.1
WESTERN ASIA	**38**	**67.7 / 72.2**						**38**	**55**	**34**	
Iraq	79	58.4 / 62.1	300	109 / 90	87 / 73	54 / 36	16 / 36	37	50	33	
Israel	5	78.7 / 82.9	4	109 / 111	100 / 99	93 / 92		14	68	52	0.2 / 0.1
Jordan	19	70.9 / 74.6	62	96 / 98	97 / 96	88 / 90	5 / 15	25	56	41	
Kuwait	8	76.1 / 79.9	4	97 / 96	95 / 97	87 / 91	19 / 26	13	52	39	
Lebanon	22	69.9 / 74.3	150	96 / 93	88 / 94	78 / 85		25	58	34	0.2 / 0.1
Occupied Palestinian Territory	17	71.9 / 75.1		82 / 3		91 / 97	3 / 12	79	50	39	

Monitoring ICPD Goals – Selected Indicators

	Indicators of Mortality			Indicators of Education				Reproductive Health Indicators			
	Infant mortality Total per 1,000 live births	Life expectancy M/F	Maternal mortality ratio	Primary enrolment (gross) M/F	Proportion reaching grade 5 M/F	Secondary enrolment (gross) M/F	% Illiterate (>15 years) M/F	Births per 1,000 women aged 15-19	Contraceptive Prevalence Any method	Modern methods	HIV prevalence rate (%) (15-49) M/F
Oman	12	74.3 / 77.6	64	82 / 83	100 / 100	90 / 87	13 / 26	10	24	18	
Saudi Arabia	19	71.0 / 75.4	18	103 / 100	100 / 93	98 / 90	12 / 24	28	32	29	
Syrian Arab Republic	16	72.4 / 76.2	130	129 / 123	93 / 92	72 / 68	12 / 26	35	58	43	
Turkey (10)	27	69.5 / 74.4	44	96 / 92	89 / 90	86 / 71	5 / 20	38	71	43	
United Arab Emirates	8	77.2 / 81.5	37	104 / 103	98 / 100	89 / 91	11 / 12	18	28	24	
Yemen	58	61.3 / 64.6	430	100 / 74	67 / 65	61 / 30	27 / 65	71	23	13	
ARAB STATES (11)	**44.0**	**66.7 / 70.3**	**495**	**103 / 92**	**88 / 86**	**71 / 65**	**24 / 45**	**36**	**39**	**31**	**0.5 / <0.1**
EUROPE	**8**	**70.6 / 78.9**						**18**	**68**	**53**	
EASTERN EUROPE	**13**	**63.0 / 74.5**						**26**	**68**	**45**	
Bulgaria	12	69.6 / 76.8	11	101 / 100		108 / 104	1 / 2	40	42	26	
Czech Republic	4	73.4 / 79.6	4	100 / 100	100 / 100	96 / 97		11	72	63	<0.1 / <0.1
Hungary	7	69.4 / 77.5	6	98 / 96		96 / 95	1 / 1	19	77	68	0.1 / <0.1
Poland	7	71.5 / 79.8	8	98 / 97		100 / 99	7 / 7	13	49	19	0.1 / 0.1
Romania	15	69.1 / 76.2	24	105 / 104		86 / 86	2 / 4	32	70	38	0.1 / 0.1
Slovakia	7	70.9 / 78.6	6	101 / 99		94 / 95		20	74	41	
NORTHERN EUROPE (12)	**5**	**76.5 / 81.5**						**19**	**77**	**72**	
Denmark	4	76.1 / 80.7	3	99 / 99	93 / 93	122 / 126		6	78	72	0.3 / 0.1
Estonia	7	66.0 / 76.9	25	100 / 98	97 / 97	99 / 101	0 / 0	21	70	56	2.0 / 0.6
Finland	4	76.3 / 82.5	7	98 / 98	99 / 100	109 / 114		9	77	75	0.1 / <0.1
Ireland	5	76.5 / 81.4	1	104 / 103	97 / 100	108 / 116		16	89		0.3 / 0.1
Latvia	10	67.5 / 77.8	10	96 / 93		98 / 99	0 / 0	14	48	39	1.2 / 0.4
Lithuania	8	67.6 / 78.4	11	95 / 94		99 / 99	0 / 0	19	47	31	0.2 / 0.1
Norway	3	77.9 / 82.6	7	98 / 98	100 / 100	113 / 113		8	74	69	0.2 / 0.1
Sweden	3	78.8 / 83.1	3	96 / 95		104 / 103		5	75	65	0.1 / 0.1
United Kingdom	5	77.2 / 81.7	8	107 / 107		104 / 106		24	84	82	0.3 / 0.1
SOUTHERN EUROPE (13)	**6**	**76.5 / 82.4**						**11**	**62**	**45**	
Albania	19	73.6 / 79.9	92	106 / 105		78 / 75	1 / 2	16	75	8	
Bosnia and Herzegovina	12	72.2 / 77.5	3				1 / 6	20	36	11	
Croatia	6	72.4 / 79.2	7	99 / 99		90 / 93	1 / 3	13			
Greece	7	77.2 / 81.9	3	102 / 102	97 / 100	104 / 102	2 / 6	9	76	42	0.2 / 0.1
Italy	5	77.6 / 83.5	3	104 / 103	99 / 100	101 / 100	1 / 2	6	60	39	0.6 / 0.2
Macedonia (Former Yugoslav Republic of)	15	71.9 / 76.7	10	98 / 98		85 / 83	2 / 6	21	14	10	
Montenegro	22	72.4 / 76.8						17	39	17	
Portugal	5	75.1 / 81.3	11	118 / 112		94 / 102	0 / 1	14	67	63	0.7 / 0.3
Serbia	12	71.8 / 76.4	14[14]	97 / 97[14]		87 / 89	1 / 6[14]	25	41	19	0.2 / 0.1
Slovenia	5	74.2 / 81.6	6	101 / 100		96 / 95	0 / 0	7	74	59	
Spain	4	77.7 / 84.3	4	106 / 104	100 / 100	115 / 122	2 / 4	9	66	62	0.8 / 0.2
WESTERN EUROPE (15)	**4**	**77.0 / 82.9**						**8**	**70**	**67**	
Austria	4	77.0 / 82.7	4	102 / 101		104 / 100		12	51	47	0.3 / 0.1
Belgium	4	76.5 / 82.4	8	102 / 102	96 / 97	112 / 108		7	78	74	0.3 / 0.1
France	4	77.2 / 84.2	8	110 / 109	98 / 98	114 / 114		7	71	71	0.5 / 0.2
Germany	4	76.6 / 82.2	4	103 / 103		102 / 100		9	70	66	0.2 / 0.1
Netherlands	5	77.6 / 81.9	6	108 / 105	99 / 100	119 / 117		5	67	65	0.3 / 0.1
Switzerland	4	79.1 / 84.2	5	98 / 97		95 / 90		4	82	78	0.7 / 0.5
LATIN AMERICA & CARIBBEAN	**21**	**70.2 / 76.7**						**76**	**72**	**64**	
CARIBBEAN (16)	**28**	**69.0 / 74.3**						**64**	**59**	**55**	
Cuba	5	76.3 / 80.5	45	102 / 100	96 / 98	93 / 94	0 / 0	47	73	72	0.1 / 0.1

	Indicators of Mortality			Indicators of Education				Reproductive Health Indicators			
	Infant mortality Total per 1,000 live births	Life expectancy M/F	Maternal mortality ratio	Primary enrolment (gross) M/F	Proportion reaching grade 5 M/F	Secondary enrolment (gross) M/F	% Illiterate (>15 years) M/F	Births per 1,000 women aged 15-19	Contraceptive Prevalence Any method	Modern methods	HIV prevalence rate (%) (15-49) M/F
Dominican Republic	29	69.4 / 75.6	150	101 / 96	66 / 71	63 / 75	13 / 13	108	61	60	1.0 / 1.1
Haiti	48	59.2 / 63.0	670				43 / 40	46	32	25	2.1 / 2.3
Jamaica	13	70.0 / 75.3	170	95 / 95	88 / 93	86 / 89	26 / 14	78	69	66	2.3 / 0.9
Puerto Rico	7	74.9 / 82.8	18				4 / 8	47	84	72	
Trinidad and Tobago	12	68.0 / 71.9	45	96 / 94	90 / 92	75 / 78	1 / 2	35	38	33	1.2 / 1.8
CENTRAL AMERICA	19	72.5 / 77.8						74	69	64	
Costa Rica	10	76.5 / 81.3	30	112 / 111	93 / 95	83 / 89	5 / 5	71	80	71	0.5 / 0.2
El Salvador	21	68.9 / 75.0	170	116 / 112	70 / 74	63 / 66		81	67	61	1.2 / 0.5
Guatemala	29	66.9 / 73.9	290	118 / 109	70 / 68	56 / 51	25 / 37	107	43	34	1.1 / 0.4
Honduras	28	67.0 / 73.8	280	119 / 118	81 / 87	66 / 86	20 / 20	93	65	56	0.9 / 0.4
Mexico	16	73.9 / 78.7	60	114 / 111	94 / 95	86 / 88	8 / 10	65	71	67	0.4 / 0.2
Nicaragua	21	70.1 / 76.2	170	117 / 115	50 / 57	62 / 70	23 / 23	113	72	70	0.3 / 0.1
Panama	18	73.1 / 78.3	130	113 / 110	87 / 89	67 / 73	7 / 9	83			1.4 / 0.6
SOUTH AMERICA (17)	21	69.6 / 76.5						78	74	66	
Argentina	13	71.7 / 79.2	77	113 / 112	89 / 91	80 / 89	3 / 3	57	65		0.8 / 0.3
Bolivia	45	63.6 / 67.9	290	109 / 109	85 / 85	84 / 81	7 / 19	78	58	35	0.2 / 0.1
Brazil	23	68.9 / 76.2	110	146 / 135		101 / 111	12 / 11	89	77	70	0.4 / 0.2
Chile	7	75.6 / 81.6	16	107 / 102	99 / 99	90 / 92	4 / 4	60	64		0.4 / 0.2
Colombia	19	69.4 / 76.7	130	117 / 115	78 / 86	78 / 87	7 / 7	65	78	68	0.8 / 0.3
Ecuador	21	72.2 / 78.1	210	117 / 117	77 / 78	67 / 68	8 / 10	83	73	58	0.5 / 0.2
Paraguay	32	69.8 / 74.0	150	113 / 110	86 / 90	66 / 67	6 / 8	72	73	61	0.8 / 0.3
Peru	21	69.1 / 74.2	240	116 / 117	90 / 89	93 / 96	6 / 18	60	71	48	0.6 / 0.3
Uruguay	13	72.9 / 79.9	20	117 / 113	92 / 95	94 / 109	4 / 3	61	77	75	0.8 / 0.3
Venezuela (Bolivarian Republic of)	17	70.9 / 76.9	57	106 / 103	90 / 95	73 / 82	7 / 7	90	70	62	1.1 / 0.4
NORTHERN AMERICA (18)	6	75.9 / 81.1						40	73	69	
Canada	5	78.4 / 83.0	7	100 / 99		119 / 116		15	74		0.5 / 0.2
United States of America	6	75.7 / 80.9	11	98 / 99	96 / 98	94 / 94		42	73	68	0.9 / 0.3
OCEANIA	26	72.8 / 78.0						27	58	52	
AUSTRALIA-NEW ZEALAND	4	78.9 / 83.4						16	72	66	
Australia (19)	4	79.0 / 83.7	4	105 / 105		154 / 146		14	71		0.3 / <0.1
Melanesia (20)	55	57.1 / 62.6						48	28	20	
New Zealand	5	78.3 / 82.2	9	102 / 102		117 / 123		23	74	71	0.1 / <0.1
Papua New Guinea	60	54.7 / 60.4	470	60 / 50			37 / 49	51	26	20	1.8 / 1.2
COUNTRIES WITH ECONOMIES IN TRANSITION OF THE FORMER USSR (21)											
Armenia	29	68.5 / 75.2	76	96 / 100		88 / 91	0 / 1	30	53	20	0.2 / 0.1
Azerbaijan	72	63.9 / 71.3	82	98 / 95		85 / 81	0 / 2	29	55	12	0.3 / 0.1
Belarus	9	63.2 / 75.3	18	97 / 95		95 / 97	0 / 1	22	73	57	0.3 / 0.1
Georgia	39	67.1 / 74.8	66	94 / 97	86 / 90	83 / 86		30	47	27	0.2 / 0.1
Kazakhstan	24	61.9 / 72.6	140	105 / 106		93 / 92	0 / 1	31	51	49	0.2 / 0.1
Kyrgyzstan	53	62.1 / 70.0	150	97 / 96		86 / 87	1 / 2	31	48	45	0.2 / 0.1
Republic of Moldova	16	65.2 / 72.5	22	97 / 96		87 / 91	0 / 1	32	68	44	0.6 / 0.2
Russian Federation	16	58.9 / 72.6	28	96 / 96		85 / 83	0 / 1	28	73	53	1.7 / 0.6
Tajikistan	59	64.2 / 69.5	170	103 / 98		90 / 75	0 / 1	28	38	33	0.4 / 0.1
Turkmenistan	74	59.1 / 67.6	130				1 / 2	16	62	53	
Ukraine	13	62.2 / 73.8	18	102 / 102		94 / 93	0 / 1	28	68	38	1.9 / 1.3
Uzbekistan	55	64.1 / 70.5	24	97 / 94		103 / 102	2 / 4	34	65	59	0.1 / 0.1

Demographic, Social and Economic Indicators

	Total population (millions) (2008)	Projected population (millions) (2050)	Ave. pop. growth rate (%) (2005-2010)	% urban (2008)	Urban growth rate (2005-2010)	Population/ ha arable & perm. crop land	Total fertility rate (2008)	% births with skilled atten-dants	GNI per capita PPP$ (2006)	Expen-ditures/ primary student (% of GDP per capita)	Health expen-ditures, public (% of GDP)	External population assistance (US$,000)	Under-5 mortality M/F estimates for 2008	Per capita energy con-sumption	Access to im-proved drinking water sources
World Total	6,749.7	9,191.3	1.2	50	2.0		2.54	66	9,209				73 / 72	1,796	83
More developed regions (*)	1,226.3	1,245.2	0.3	75	0.5		1.60	100					9 / 8		
Less developed regions (+)	5,523.4	7,946.0	1.4	44	2.5		2.73	62					80 / 80		
Least developed countries (‡)	823.8	1,742.0	2.4	28	4.1		4.60	35	1,076				145 / 133	312	
AFRICA (1)	987.0	1,997.9	2.3	39	3.3		4.63	47				2,310,570[22]	148 / 135		
EASTERN AFRICA	315.8	692.9	2.5	23	3.9		5.21	34				1,259,919	140 / 125		
Burundi	8.9	28.3	3.9	10	6.8	5.3	6.79	34	320	19.1	1.0	11,942	178 / 156		79
Eritrea	5.0	11.5	3.2	21	5.4	5.4	5.00	28	680	11.3	1.7	9,974	79 / 72		60
Ethiopia	85.2	183.4	2.5	17	4.3	4.6	5.24	6	630		3.0	233,235	151 / 136	288	22
Kenya	38.6	84.8	2.7	22	4.0	4.6	4.92	42	1,470	23.6	2.1	169,437	111 / 95	484	61
Madagascar	20.2	44.5	2.7	29	3.8	3.8	4.72	51	870	8.4	2.0	13,038	110 / 99		46
Malawi	14.3	31.9	2.6	19	5.2	3.6	5.55	54	690	13.5	8.7	76,443	134 / 125		73
Mauritius (2)	1.3	1.4	0.8	42	0.9	1.1	1.86	99	10,640	11.8	2.2	794	18 / 14		100
Mozambique	21.8	39.1	2.0	37	4.1	3.3	5.06	48	660	14.1	2.7	136,904	170 / 153	497	43
Rwanda	10.0	22.6	2.8	18	4.2	5.6	5.86	28	730	11.3	4.1	67,329	199 / 173		74
Somalia	9.0	21.1	2.9	37	4.2	4.1	6.00	33				8,854	196 / 186		29
Uganda	31.9	92.9	3.2	13	4.4	2.9	6.42	42	880	11.3	2.0	174,668	132 / 119		60
United Republic of Tanzania	41.5	85.1	2.5	25	4.2	2.8	5.11	43	980		2.9	160,011	123 / 110	530	62
Zambia	12.2	22.9	1.9	35	2.3	1.4	5.13	43	1,140	5.4	2.7	148,100	163 / 147	621	58
Zimbabwe	13.5	19.1	1.0	37	2.2	2.3	3.15	69			3.6	49,190	100 / 86	741	81
MIDDLE AFRICA (3)	122.5	312.7	2.8	42	4.3		5.99	55				164,835	200 / 178		
Angola	17.5	44.6	2.8	57	4.4	3.2	6.40	45	3,890		1.5	30,640	243 / 215	615	53
Cameroon	18.9	33.1	2.0	57	3.5	1.2	4.27	63	2,060	10.3	1.5	19,445	150 / 136	392	66
Central African Republic	4.4	7.6	1.8	39	2.3	1.4	4.54	54	690	11.8	1.5	12,268	178 / 145		75
Chad	11.1	29.4	2.9	27	4.7	1.7	6.16	14	1,170	7.3	1.5	8,325	195 / 180		42
Congo, Democratic Republic of the (4)	64.7	186.8	3.2	34	5.1	4.6	6.69	61	270		1.5	90,486	205 / 184	289	46
Congo, Republic of	3.8	7.6	2.1	61	2.7	2.4	4.44	86		4.0	0.9	1,429	112 / 89	332	58
Gabon	1.4	2.1	1.5	85	2.1	0.8	3.03	86	11,180		3.0	2,242	89 / 79	1,333	88
NORTHERN AFRICA (5)	199.5	310.2	1.7	51	2.4		2.86	71				108,269[23]	55 / 46		
Algeria	34.4	49.6	1.5	65	2.5	0.9	2.36	95	5,940	11.3	2.6	3,485	34 / 30	1,058	85
Egypt	76.8	121.2	1.8	43	1.8	6.9	2.87	74	4,940		2.3	38,679	37 / 29	841	98
Libyan Arab Jamahiriya	6.3	9.7	2.0	78	2.2	0.1	2.69	100	11,630		2.2	536	20 / 19	3,218	
Morocco	31.6	42.6	1.2	56	1.8	1.1	2.35	63	3,860	22.9	1.9	16,832	42 / 28	458	81
Sudan	39.4	73.0	2.2	43	4.3	1.1	4.17	49	1,780		1.4	43,513	110 / 96	499	70
Tunisia	10.4	13.2	1.1	67	1.7	0.5	1.91	90	6,490	24.1	2.4	5,224	23 / 21	843	93
SOUTHERN AFRICA	56.0	65.0	0.6	58	1.5		2.69	89				305,785	74 / 63		
Botswana	1.9	2.7	1.2	60	2.5	2.1	2.87	99	11,730	17.2	4.5	27,676	73 / 60	1,032	95
Lesotho	2.0	2.4	0.6	25	3.5	2.3	3.33	55	1,810	24.2	8.5	10,647	104 / 90		79
Namibia	2.1	3.0	1.3	37	2.9	1.1	3.15	76	4,770	20.1	3.5	70,474	70 / 58	683	87
South Africa	48.8	55.6	0.6	61	1.4	0.4	2.62	92	8,900	14.2	3.6	183,967	71 / 60	2,722	88
Swaziland	1.1	1.4	0.6	25	1.7	1.8	3.41	74	4,700	12.4	4.0	13,022	121 / 103		62
WESTERN AFRICA (6)	293.2	617.0	2.4	43	3.8		5.25	41				471,763	179 / 170		
Benin	9.3	22.5	3.0	41	4.0	1.4	5.37	78	1,250	11.5	3.0	23,852	147 / 143	304	67
Burkina Faso	15.2	37.5	2.9	20	5.0	2.6	5.96	54	1,130	34.7	4.0	30,648	183 / 176		61
Côte d'Ivoire	19.6	34.7	1.8	49	3.2	1.1	4.40	57	1,580		0.8	35,229	192 / 173	422	84
Gambia	1.8	3.6	2.6	57	4.2	3.5	4.65	57	1,110	7.4	3.4	3,090	129 / 124		82

	Total population (millions) (2008)	Projected population (millions) (2050)	Ave. pop. growth rate (%) (2005-2010)	% urban (2008)	Urban growth rate (2005-2010)	Population/ ha arable & perm. crop land	Total fertility rate (2008)	% births with skilled atten-dants	GNI per capita PPP$ (2006)	Expen-ditures/ primary student (% of GDP per capita)	Health expen-ditures, public (% of GDP)	External population assistance (US$,000)	Under-5 mortality M/F estimates for 2008	Per capita energy con-sumption	Access to im-proved drinking water sources
Ghana	23.9	41.9	2.0	50	3.5	1.9	3.79	50	1,240	12.8	2.1	53,639	90 / 86	397	75
Guinea	9.6	22.7	2.2	34	3.5	3.9	5.39	38	1,130		0.7	13,184	163 / 144		50
Guinea-Bissau	1.7	5.3	3.0	30	3.3	2.4	7.04	39	460		1.7	2,342	204 / 181		59
Liberia	3.9	12.5	4.5	60	5.7	3.7	6.75	51	260		4.4	7,069	212 / 194		61
Mali	12.7	34.2	3.0	32	4.8	1.9	6.46	41	1,000		2.9	31,466	206 / 189		50
Mauritania	3.2	6.4	2.5	41	3.0	3.0	4.32	57	1,970	9.8	1.7	4,869	98 / 85		53
Niger	14.7	53.2	3.5	16	4.0	0.8	7.16	18	630	19.0	1.9	12,633	183 / 188		46
Nigeria	151.5	288.7	2.3	48	3.8	1.2	5.27	35	1,410		1.2	209,913	190 / 182	734	48
Senegal	12.7	25.3	2.5	42	3.1	3.3	4.63	52	1,560	18.7	1.7	25,804	120 / 108	258	76
Sierra Leone	6.0	13.5	2.0	38	2.9	4.9	6.44	43	610		1.9	8,437	290 / 264		57
Togo	6.8	14.1	2.7	42	4.3	1.3	4.74	62	770	6.7	1.4	9,587	134 / 116	320	52
ASIA	**4,075.4**	**5,265.9**	**1.1**	**41**	**2.5**		**2.33**	**65**				**929,713**	**56 / 61**		
EASTERN ASIA (7)	**1,546.9**	**1,591.2**	**0.5**	**47**	**2.2**		**1.68**	**98**				**63,405[23,24]**	**23 / 32**		
China	1,336.3	1,408.8	0.6	43	2.7	5.4	1.73	98	4,660		1.8	57,521	24 / 34	1,316	77
Democratic People's Republic of Korea	23.9	24.7	0.3	63	0.9	2.1	1.85	97			3.0	969	62 / 62	898	100
Hong Kong SAR, China (8)	7.3	9.0	1.0	100	1.0		0.96	100	39,200	14.9			5 / 4	2,653	
Japan	127.9	102.5	0.0	66	0.2	0.8	1.27	100	32,840	22.6	6.7	(371,241)	5 / 4	4,152	100
Mongolia	2.7	3.4	1.0	57	1.2	0.5	1.86	99	2,810	14.3	3.3	4,764	57 / 49		62
Republic of Korea	48.4	42.3	0.3	81	0.6	1.7	1.20	100	22,990	18.6	3.1	151	5 / 5	4,426	92
SOUTH-EASTERN ASIA	**579.9**	**766.6**	**1.3**	**47**	**3.0**		**2.31**	**70**				**355,904**	**39 / 30**		
Cambodia	14.7	25.1	1.7	22	4.6	2.5	3.13	44	1,550	6.1	1.5	47,122	92 / 84		41
Indonesia	234.3	296.9	1.2	52	3.3	2.5	2.16	66	3,310	2.6	1.0	155,125	36 / 26	814	77
Lao People's Democratic Republic	6.0	9.3	1.7	31	5.6	4.0	3.15	19	1,740	8.6	0.7	9,882	69 / 62		51
Malaysia	27.0	39.0	1.7	70	3.0	0.5	2.57	100	12,160	18.6	1.9	381	12 / 10	2,389	99
Myanmar	49.2	58.7	0.9	33	2.9	3.0	2.04	57			2.7	0.3	8,771	105 / 87	307	78
Philippines	89.7	140.5	1.9	65	3.0	2.9	3.20	60	3,430	11.7	1.2	47,541	32 / 21	528	85
Singapore	4.5	5.0	1.2	100	1.2	5.0	1.26	100	43,300		1.1		4 / 4	6,933	100
Thailand	64.3	67.4	0.7	33	1.7	1.6	1.85	97	7,440	13.9	2.2	45,630	17 / 13	1,588	99
Timor-Leste, Democratic Republic of	1.2	3.5	3.5	27	5.0	4.6	6.48	19	5,100		11.9	5,760	90 / 89		58
Viet Nam	88.5	120.0	1.3	28	3.1	6.2	2.12	88	2,310		1.5	75,690	26 / 19	617	85
SOUTH CENTRAL ASIA	**1,724.6**	**2,536.0**	**1.5**	**32**	**2.5**		**2.86**	**47**				**371,544**	**77 / 85**		
Afghanistan	28.2	79.4	3.9	24	5.4	2.0	7.03	14			1.0	45,621	232 / 237		39
Bangladesh	161.3	254.1	1.7	27	3.5	9.3	2.81	20	1,230	7.0	0.8	87,072	68 / 67	158	74
Bhutan	0.7	0.9	1.4	35	4.9	3.4	2.17	51	4,000		2.8	4,289	67 / 58		62
India	1,186.2	1,658.3	1.5	29	2.4	3.4	2.78	47	2,460	11.1	1.0	141,359	73 / 83	491	86
Iran (Islamic Republic of)	72.2	100.2	1.4	69	2.1	0.9	2.02	97	9,800	9.7	4.4	3,503	35 / 34	2,352	94
Nepal	28.8	51.9	2.0	17	4.9	10.1	3.24	19	1,010	12.4	1.6	52,797	68 / 72	338	90
Pakistan	167.0	292.2	1.8	36	3.0	3.5	3.46	54	2,410	7.0	0.4	29,884	89 / 99	490	91
Sri Lanka	19.4	18.7	0.5	15	0.5	4.5	1.88	97	3,730		1.9	7,019	14 / 12	477	79
WESTERN ASIA	**224.0**	**372.0**	**1.8**	**66**	**2.2**		**2.97**	**79**				**138,861[25]**	**52 / 44**		
Iraq	29.5	61.9	1.8	67	1.7	0.4	4.21	89			3.1	61,211	105 / 98		81
Israel	7.0	10.5	1.7	92	1.7	0.4	2.73		23,840	22.8	4.8		6 / 5	2,816	100
Jordan	6.1	10.1	3.0	78	3.1	2.0	3.08	100	4,820	14.0	4.8	3,007	23 / 19	1,311	97
Kuwait	2.9	5.2	2.4	98	2.5	1.6	2.17	100			12.2	1.7		11 / 9	11,100	
Lebanon	4.1	5.2	1.1	87	1.2	0.3	2.19	98	9,600	7.2	3.8	5,543	30 / 20	1,391	100
Occupied Palestinian Territory	4.1	10.3	3.2	72	3.3	1.7	5.04	99				8,785	22 / 17		92

Demographic, Social and Economic Indicators

	Total population (millions) (2008)	Projected population (millions) (2050)	Ave. pop. growth rate (%) (2005-2010)	% urban (2008)	Urban growth rate (2005-2010)	Population/ ha arable & perm. crop land	Total fertility rate (2008)	% births with skilled atten-dants	GNI per capita PPP$ (2006)	Expen-ditures/ primary student (% of GDP per capita)	Health expen-ditures, public (% of GDP)	External population assistance (US$,000)	Under-5 mortality M/F estimates for 2008	Per capita energy con-sumption	Access to im-proved drinking water sources
Oman	2.7	4.6	2.0	72	2.0	7.7	2.95	98		16.3	2.1	6	14 / 13	5,570	
Saudi Arabia	25.3	45.0	2.2	82	2.5	0.4	3.30	96	22,300		2.6	317	26 / 17	6,068	
Syrian Arab Republic	20.4	34.9	2.5	54	3.1	0.8	3.04	93	4,110	14.2	2.1	3,367	20 / 15	948	93
Turkey (10)	75.8	98.9	1.3	69	2.0	0.8	2.13	83	8,410	11.8	5.4	32,728	35 / 26	1,182	96
United Arab Emirates	4.5	8.5	2.9	78	2.9	0.6	2.28	100		7.1	1.9		9 / 9	11,436	100
Yemen	23.1	58.0	3.0	31	4.9	5.8	5.44	20	2,090		2.1	23,896	83 / 72	319	67
ARAB STATES (11)	337.3	586.3	2.0	56	2.5	2.7	3.3	71	5,978	11.2	2.3	228,124	62 / 53	1,646	84
EUROPE	731.1	664.2	0.0	72	0.2		1.45	100					11 / 9		
EASTERN EUROPE	293.6	221.7	-0.5	68	-0.4		1.29	100				5,826	19 / 14		
Bulgaria	7.6	4.9	-0.7	71	-0.3	0.1	1.31	99	10,270	19.0	4.7	323	16 / 12	2,592	99
Czech Republic	10.2	8.8	0.0	73	0.0	0.2	1.24	100	20,920	12.9	6.3		5 / 4	4,417	100
Hungary	10.0	8.5	-0.3	68	0.3	0.2	1.28	100	16,970	21.9	5.5		9 / 8	2,752	99
Poland	38.0	30.3	-0.2	61	-0.3	0.5	1.22	100	14,250	22.9	4.3	10	8 / 7	2,436	
Romania	21.3	15.9	-0.5	54	-0.1	0.2	1.30	99	10,150		3.9	5,493	20 / 15	1,772	57
Slovakia	5.4	4.7	0.0	56	0.2	0.3	1.25	100	17,060	13.0	5.2		9 / 8	3,496	100
NORTHERN EUROPE (12)	97.6	108.2	0.4	84	0.5		1.78	99					6 / 6		
Denmark	5.5	5.5	0.2	87	0.5	0.1	1.80		36,190	25.5	7.7	(103,910)	6 / 6	3,621	100
Estonia	1.3	1.1	-0.4	69	-0.3	0.2	1.49	100	18,090	20.1	3.8		11 / 8	3,786	100
Finland	5.3	5.4	0.3	63	0.8	0.1	1.83	100	33,170	18.7	5.8	(50,948)	5 / 4	6,664	100
Ireland	4.4	6.2	1.8	61	2.3	0.3	1.96	100	34,730	13.9	6.5	(143,654)	6 / 6	3,676	
Latvia	2.3	1.8	-0.5	68	-0.5	0.2	1.29	100	14,840	20.6	3.9		16 / 11	2,050	99
Lithuania	3.4	2.7	-0.5	67	-0.4	0.2	1.26	100	149,550	14.4	4.0		13 / 9	2,515	
Norway	4.7	5.7	0.6	77	0.7	0.2	1.84		50,070	21.7	7.5	(114,775)	4 / 4	6,948	100
Sweden	9.2	10.5	0.5	85	0.5	0.1	1.80		34,310	24.0	7.5	(369,569)	4 / 4	5,782	100
United Kingdom	61.0	68.7	0.4	90	0.5	0.2	1.82	99	33,650	18.4	7.1	(863,793)	6 / 6	3,884	100
SOUTHERN EUROPE (13)	152.1	146.3	0.3	67	0.7		1.43	99				13,324	8 / 7		
Albania	3.2	3.5	0.6	47	1.9	2.0	2.04	100	6,000	7.8	2.6	4,055	24 / 20	762	96
Bosnia and Herzegovina	3.9	3.2	0.1	47	1.4	0.1	1.23	100	6,780		5.2	3,861	15 / 13	1,268	97
Croatia	4.6	3.7	-0.1	57	0.4	0.2	1.35	100	13,850	20.2	6.0	1,644	8 / 7	2,000	100
Greece	11.2	10.8	0.2	61	0.6	0.4	1.33		30,870	16.1	4.3	(13,641)	8 / 8	2,790	
Italy	58.9	54.6	0.1	68	0.4	0.2	1.38	99	28,970	25.9	6.8	(3,904)	6 / 6	3,160	
Macedonia (Former Yugoslav Republic of)	2.0	1.7	0.1	67	0.8	0.3	1.42	98	7,850	23.8	5.5	3,659	17 / 16	1,346	
Montenegro	0.6	0.6	-0.3	60	-0.8		1.83	99	8,930		6.2	1,392	25 / 23		
Portugal	10.7	10.0	0.4	59	1.4	0.7	1.46	100	19,960	24.4	7.4	(6,807)	7 / 7	2,575	
Serbia	9.9	9.6	0.1	52	0.5	0.4[14]	1.80	99	9,320		5.8	5,829	14 / 13		93[14]
Slovenia	2.0	1.7	0.0	48	-0.6	0.1	1.28	100	23,970	30.0	6.2		6 / 6	3,657	
Spain	44.6	46.4	0.8	77	1.0	0.1	1.42		28,200	18.6	5.9	(67,452)	6 / 5	3,346	100
WESTERN EUROPE (15)	187.9	188.0	0.2	77	0.4		1.59	100					6 / 5		
Austria	8.4	8.5	0.4	67	0.7	0.2	1.42		36,040	23.2	7.7	(7,959)	6 / 5	4,174	100
Belgium	10.5	10.6	0.2	97	0.3	0.2	1.65	99	33,860	20.2	6.9	(75,677)	6 / 5	5,407	
France	61.9	68.3	0.5	77	0.8	0.1	1.89	99	32,240	17.6	8.9	(250,720)	6 / 5	4,534	100
Germany	82.5	74.1	-0.1	74	0.1	0.1	1.36	100	32,680	16.6	8.2	(151,949)	5 / 5	4,180	100
Netherlands	16.5	17.2	0.2	82	0.9	0.5	1.72	100	37,940	18.7	6.0	(546,801)	6 / 6	5,015	100
Switzerland	7.5	8.4	0.4	73	0.5	1.0	1.42	100	40,840	24.9	6.8	(36,540)	6 / 5	3,651	100
LATIN AMERICA & CARIBBEAN	579.4	769.2	1.2	79	1.7		2.35	89				316,094	30 / 23		
CARIBBEAN (16)	41.6	50.4	0.9	66	1.6		2.40	73				125,582	44 / 32		
Cuba	11.3	9.9	0.0	76	0.0	0.4	1.50	100		37.6	6.9	5,116	7 / 6	906	91

	Total population (millions) (2008)	Projected population (millions) (2050)	Ave. pop. growth rate (%) (2005-2010)	% urban (2008)	Urban growth rate (2005-2010)	Population/ ha arable & perm. crop land	Total fertility rate (2008)	% births with skilled attendants	GNI per capita PPP$ (2006)	Expenditures/ primary student (% of GDP per capita)	Health expenditures, public (% of GDP)	External population assistance (US$,000)	Under-5 mortality M/F estimates for 2008	Per capita energy consumption	Access to improved drinking water sources
Dominican Republic	9.9	14.0	1.5	69	2.6	1.0	2.80	96	5,550	8.1	1.7	14,453	37 / 28	777	95
Haiti	9.8	15.3	1.6	47	4.5	5.0	3.50	26	1,070		3.2	96,668	82 / 59	269	54
Jamaica	2.7	2.8	0.5	53	0.9	1.8	2.42	97	7,050	11.5	2.3	7,397	18 / 16	1,445	93
Puerto Rico	4.0	4.4	0.6	98	0.8	0.8	1.83	100					9 / 8		
Trinidad and Tobago	1.3	1.3	0.4	13	2.9	0.8	1.64	98	16,800	15.7	2.4	1,948	20 / 15	9,599	91
CENTRAL AMERICA	**149.6**	**202.0**	**1.3**	**71**	**1.8**		**2.44**	**83**				**83,595**	**27 / 21**		
Costa Rica	4.5	6.4	1.5	63	2.3	1.4	2.08	94	9,220	17.0	5.4	1,581	13 / 10	883	97
El Salvador	7.0	10.0	1.4	61	1.9	2.2	2.66	69	5,610	9.2	3.8	9,241	32 / 26	694	84
Guatemala	13.7	27.5	2.5	49	3.4	2.8	4.11	41	5,120	6.5	2.0	14,992	44 / 33	628	95
Honduras	7.2	12.1	2.0	48	2.9	1.4	3.26	67	3,420		3.8	15,175	46 / 36	566	87
Mexico	107.8	132.3	1.1	77	1.5	0.8	2.19	94	11,990	15.5	2.9	11,322	22 / 17	1,712	97
Nicaragua	5.7	8.2	1.3	57	1.8	0.4	2.72	67	2,720	8.8	4.1	29,598	28 / 22	611	79
Panama	3.4	5.1	1.7	73	2.8	0.9	2.55	91	8,690	9.6	5.0	1,686	27 / 20	804	90
SOUTH AMERICA (17)	**388.2**	**516.8**	**1.3**	**83**	**1.7**		**2.31**	**93**				**106,918**	**30 / 23**		
Argentina	39.9	51.4	1.0	92	1.2	0.1	2.24	99	11,670	10.9	4.5	5,602	17 / 13	1,644	96
Bolivia	9.7	14.9	1.8	66	2.5	1.2	3.46	67	3,810	16.2	4.3	16,779	64 / 55	578	85
Brazil	194.2	254.1	1.3	86	1.8	0.4	2.23	97	8,700	10.8	3.5	17,509	32 / 24	1,122	90
Chile	16.8	20.7	1.0	88	1.3	1.0	1.93	100	11,300	12.8	2.8	2,964	10 / 8	1,815	95
Colombia	46.7	61.9	1.3	74	1.7	2.3	2.21	96	6,130	19.5	6.2	8,307	29 / 22	636	93
Ecuador	13.5	18.0	1.1	66	2.1	1.2	2.56	80	6,810		2.1	11,128	29 / 21	799	94
Paraguay	6.2	9.9	1.8	60	2.8	0.5	3.05	77	4,040	12.6	2.7	5,189	43 / 32	674	86
Peru	28.2	39.0	1.2	71	1.3	1.0	2.49	73	6,490	6.7	2.1	35,370	30 / 26	506	83
Uruguay	3.4	3.6	0.3	92	0.4	0.2	2.11	100	9,940	6.5	3.4	538	17 / 14	875	100
Venezuela	28.1	42.0	1.7	93	2.0	0.6	2.53	95	10,970		2.1	3,534	24 / 19	2,293	83
NORTHERN AMERICA (18)	**342.1**	**445.3**	**1.0**	**82**	**1.3**		**2.00**	**100**					**8 / 8**		
Canada	33.2	42.8	0.9	80	1.0	0.0	1.52	100	36,280		6.8	(300,868)	6 / 6	8,417	100
United States of America	308.8	402.4	1.0	82	1.3	0.0	2.05	100	44,070	21.5	7.2	(2,535,693)	8 / 8	7,893	100
OCEANIA	**34.7**	**48.7**	**1.2**	**71**	**1.3**		**2.29**	**76**				**52,325**	**37 / 32**		
AUSTRALIA-NEW ZEALAND	**25.2**	**33.3**	**1.0**	**88**	**1.2**		**1.82**	**100**					**6 / 5**		
Australia (19)	21.0	28.0	1.0	89	1.2	0.0	1.79	100	33,940	16.4	5.9	(95,463)	6 / 5	5,978	100
Melanesia (20)	8.3	13.8	1.9	19	2.0		3.59	46					81 / 69		
New Zealand	4.2	5.2	0.9	87	1.0	0.1	1.99	95	25,750	19.4	6.9	(17,663)	6 / 6	4,090	
Papua New Guinea	6.5	11.2	2.0	12	1.9	5.1	3.74	38	1,630		3.6	52,325	90 / 76		39
COUNTRIES WITH ECONOMIES IN TRANSITION OF THE FORMER USSR (21)												**105,294**			
Armenia	3.0	2.5	-0.2	64	-0.3	0.6	1.37	98	4,950		1.8	3,015	36 / 31	848	92
Azerbaijan	8.5	9.4	0.8	52	1.0	1.0	1.80	97	5,430	6.3	1.0	9,615	89 / 81	1,649	77
Belarus	9.6	7.0	-0.6	73	0.0	0.2	1.20	100	9,700	14.1	5.0	3,830	14 / 10	2,720	100
Georgia	4.4	3.1	-0.8	53	-0.6	0.7	1.40	92	3,880		1.7	9,176	45 / 37	718	82
Kazakhstan	15.5	17.3	0.7	58	1.2	0.1	2.29	100	8,700	10.0	2.5	9,324	33 / 23	3,462	86
Kyrgyzstan	5.4	6.6	1.1	36	1.6	0.9	2.45	98	1,790	7.6	2.5	7,002	69 / 58	544	77
Republic of Moldova	3.8	2.9	-0.9	42	-1.5	0.3	1.40	100	2,660	16.6	4.2	3,041	21 / 17	917	92
Russian Federation	141.8	107.8	-0.5	73	-0.6	0.1	1.34	100	12,740		3.2	4,725	24 / 18	4,517	97
Tajikistan	6.8	10.8	1.5	26	1.6	1.9	3.31	83	1,560	8.7	1.1	5,304	81 / 72	528	59
Turkmenistan	5.0	6.8	1.3	49	2.2	0.6	2.48	100			3.2	622	104 / 84	3,381	72
Ukraine	45.9	30.9	-0.8	68	-0.7	0.2	1.21	100	6,110	14.8	3.7	43,456	18 / 13	3,041	96
Uzbekistan	27.8	38.4	1.4	37	1.6	1.3	2.46	100	2,190		2.4	6,186	71 / 60	1,798	82

Selected Indicators for Less Populous Countries/Territories

Monitoring ICPD Goals Selected Indicators	Indicators of Mortality			Indicators of Education		Reproductive Health Indicators			
	Infant mortality total per 1,000 live births	Life expectancy M/F	Maternal mortality ratio	Primary enrolment (gross) M/F	Secondary enrolment (gross) M/F	Births per 1,000 women aged 15-19	Contraceptive Prevalence Any method	Modern methods	HIV prevalence rate (%) (15-49) M/F
Bahamas	13	70.9 / 76.6	16	98 / 98	91 / 91	53	62	60	4.4 / 1.6
Bahrain	11	74.4 / 77.6	32	120 / 119	100 / 104	17	62	31	
Barbados	10	74.5 / 79.9	16	104 / 102	100 / 104	42	55	53	1.8 / 0.6
Belize	16	73.3 / 79.3	52	125 / 121	77 / 81	79	56	53	1.6 / 2.5
Brunei Darussalam	5	75.0 / 79.8	13	107 / 106	96 / 100	27			
Cape Verde	24	68.4 / 74.6	210	108 / 103	75 / 86	83	61		
Comoros	48	63.2 / 67.6	400	91 / 80	40 / 30	49	26	19	0.1 / <0.1
Cyprus	6	76.6 / 81.7	10	103 / 102	96 / 97	8			
Djibouti	84	53.8 / 56.2	650	49 / 40	27 / 18	23	18	17	2.4 / 3.7
Equatorial Guinea	91	50.6 / 53.0	680	125 / 119	41 / 23	123			2.8 / 4.1
Fiji	19	66.7 / 71.2	210	101 / 99	80 / 88	32			0.1 / 0.1
French Polynesia	8	71.8 / 76.9				34			
Guadeloupe	7	76.1 / 82.3				19			
Guam	9	73.3 / 78.0				52	67	58	
Guyana	42	64.3 / 70.0	470	125 / 124	106 / 104	63	35	34	2.0 / 3.0
Iceland	3	80.3 / 83.3	4	98 / 97	108 / 111	15			0.3 / 0.1
Luxembourg	4	75.8 / 81.7	12	102 / 103	94 / 98	10			0.3 / 0.1
Maldives	33	67.7 / 69.7	120	118 / 114	76 / 84	23	39	34	<0.1 / <0.1
Malta	6	77.4 / 81.4	8	101 / 99	99 / 100	13	86	46	0.1 / 0.1
Martinique	7	76.6 / 82.4				30			
Micronesia (25)	34	70.0 / 74.3		109 / 111	80 / 86	37	49	47	
Netherlands Antilles	15	71.4 / 78.9		125 / 123	87 / 95	30			
New Caledonia	6	73.0 / 79.8				26			
Polynesia (26)	16	70.7 / 75.8				28	43	37	
Qatar	8	75.3 / 76.5	12	105 / 104	103 / 100	18	43	32	
Réunion	13	72.4 / 80.6				33	67	64	
Samoa	22	68.7 / 75.0		100 / 100	76 / 86	27			
Solomon Islands	54	62.9 / 64.4	220	102 / 98	33 / 27	41			
Suriname	28	67.0 / 73.6	72	121 / 121	66 / 90	40	42	41	3.4 / 1.4
Vanuatu	28	68.4 / 72.3		110 / 106	43 / 37	44	39	28	

Demographic, Social and Economic Indicators	Total population (thousands) (2008)	Projected population (thousands) (2050)	% urban (2008)	Urban growth rate (2005-2010)	Population/ ha arable & perm. crop land	Total fertility rate (2008)	% births with skilled attendants	GNI per capita PPP$ (2006)	Under-5 mortality M/F
Bahamas	335	449	84	1.4	0.8	2.01	99		20 / 14
Bahrain	766	1,173	89	1.8	1.0	2.27	99		14 / 14
Barbados	295	272	40	1.5	0.6	1.50	100		12 / 10
Belize	294	487	52	3.1	0.8	2.90	91	7,080	22 / 17
Brunei Darussalam	398	681	75	2.6	0.1	2.28	100	49,900	7 / 6
Cape Verde	542	1,002	60	3.5	2.0	3.33	89	2,590	38 / 19
Comoros	860	1,715	28	2.7	4.3	4.24	62	1,140	70 / 53
Cyprus	864	1,183	70	1.3	0.4	1.60	100	25,060	8 / 6
Djibouti	848	1,480	87	2.2		3.90	93	2,180	132 / 116
Equatorial Guinea	520	1,183	39	2.8	1.5	5.34	63	16,620	162 / 145
Fiji	844	910	52	1.6	1.1	2.73	99	4,450	24 / 24
French Polynesia	266	357	52	1.3		2.25	100		10 / 10
Guadeloupe	448	468	98	0.7	0.4	2.10	99		10 / 8
Guam	176	242	93	1.3		2.52	87		11 / 10
Guyana	736	477	28	-0.1	0.2	2.32	94	3,410	65 / 47
Iceland	303	355	92	0.9	3.0	2.06		33,740	4 / 4
Luxembourg	472	722	82	1.0	0.1	1.66	100	60,870	7 / 6
Maldives	311	510	38	5.3	5.1	2.59	84	4,740	41 / 41
Malta	408	428	94	0.7	0.5	1.36	100	20,990	8 / 7
Martinique	400	350	98	0.3	0.6	1.91	100		8 / 8
Micronesia (25)	560	808	68	1.6		2.66	88	6,070	41 / 42
Netherlands Antilles	194	186	93	1.6	0.1	1.86			20 / 13
New Caledonia	245	360	65	2.1	8.5	2.06	92		9 / 8
Polynesia (26)	666	850	43	1.6		3.02	99		20 / 19
Qatar	856	1,333	96	2.2	0.4	2.64	100		9 / 12
Réunion	817	1,072	93	1.6	0.5	2.35			20 / 10
Samoa	189	215	23	1.7		3.89	100	5,090	27 / 25
Solomon Islands	507	955	18	4.1	4.4	3.82	43	1,850	72 / 71
Suriname	461	426	75	1.0	1.2	2.40	71	7,720	40 / 29
Vanuatu	232	454	25	4.1		3.70	92	3,480	38 / 28

Notes for Indicators

The designations employed in this publication do not imply the expression of any opinion on the part of UNFPA (United Nations Population Fund) concerning the legal status of any country, territory or area or of its authorities, or concerning the delimitation of its frontiers or boundaries.

Data for small countries or areas, generally those with population of 200,000 or less in 1990, are not given in this table separately. They have been included in their regional population figures.

(*)   More-developed regions comprise North America, Japan, Europe and Australia-New Zealand.

(+)   Less-developed regions comprise all regions of Africa, Latin America and Caribbean, Asia (excluding Japan), and Melanesia, Micronesia and Polynesia.

(‡)   Least-developed countries according to standard United Nations designation.

(1)   Including British Indian Ocean Territory and Seychelles.

(2)   Including Agalesa, Rodrigues and St. Brandon.

(3)   Including Sao Tome and Principe.

(4)   Formerly Zaire.

(5)   Including Western Sahara.

(6)   Including St. Helena, Ascension and Tristan da Cunha.

(7)   Including Macau.

(8)   On 1 July 1997, Hong Kong became a Special Administrative Region (SAR) of China.

(9)   This entry is included in the more developed regions aggregate but not in the estimate for the geographical region.

(10)   Turkey is included in Western Asia for geographical reasons. Other classifications include this country in Europe.

(11)   Comprising Algeria, Bahrain, Comoros, Djibouti, Egypt, Iraq, Jordan, Kuwait, Lebanon, Libyan Arab Jamahiriya, Mauritania, Morocco, Occupied Palestinian Territory, Oman, Qatar, Saudi Arabia, Somalia, Sudan, Syria, Tunisia, United Arab Emirates and Yemen. Regional aggregation for demographic indicators provided by the UN Population Division. Aggregations for other indicators are weighted averages based on countries with available data.

(12)   Including Channel Islands, Faeroe Islands and Isle of Man.

(13)   Including Andorra, Gibraltar, Holy See and San Marino.

(14)   Data were not available for Serbia and Montenegro separately, so the aggregate values are presented here. Following the Declaration of Independence adopted by the National Assembly of Montenegro on 3 June 2006, the membership of former Serbia and Montenegro in the United Nations was continued by Serbia, and, on 28 June 2006, Montenegro was admitted as the 192nd Member State of the United Nations.

(15)   Including Leichtenstein and Monaco.

(16)   Including Anguilla, Antigua and Barbuda, Aruba, British Virgin Islands, Cayman Islands, Dominica, Grenada, Montserrat, Netherlands Antilles, Saint Kitts and Nevis, Saint Lucia, Saint Vincent and the Grenadines, Turks and Caicos Islands, and United States Virgin Islands.

(17)   Including Falkland Islands (Malvinas) and French Guiana.

(18)   Including Bermuda, Greenland, and St. Pierre and Miquelon.

(19)   Including Christmas Island, Cocos (Keeling) Islands and Norfolk Island.

(20)   Including New Caledonia and Vanuatu.

(21)   The successor States of the former USSR are grouped under existing regions. Eastern Europe includes Belarus, Republic of Moldova, Russian Federation and Ukraine. Western Asia includes Armenia, Azerbaijan and Georgia. South Central Asia includes Kazakhstan, Kyrgyzstan, Tajikistan, Turkmenistan and Uzbekistan. Regional total, excluding subregion reported separately below.

(22)   Regional total, excluding subregion reported separately below.

(23)   These subregions are included in the UNFPA Arab States and Europe region.

(24)   Total for Eastern Europe includes some South European Balkan States and Northern European Baltic States.

(25)   Comprising Federated States of Micronesia, Guam, Kiribati, Marshall Islands, Nauru, Northern Mariana Islands, and Pacific Islands (Palau).

(26)   Comprising American Samoa, Cook Islands, Johnston Island, Pitcairn, Samoa, Tokelau, Tonga, Midway Islands, Tuvalu, and Wallis and Futuna Islands.

Technical Notes

The statistical tables in this year's *The State of World Population* report once again give special attention to indicators that can help track progress in meeting the quantitative and qualitative goals of the International Conference on Population and Development (ICPD) and the Millennium Development Goals (MDGs) in the areas of mortality reduction, access to education, access to reproductive health services including family planning, and HIV and AIDS prevalence among young people. The sources for the indicators and their rationale for selection follow, by category.

Monitoring ICPD Goals

INDICATORS OF MORTALITY

Infant mortality, male and female life expectancy at birth.
Source: Spreadsheets provided by the United Nations Population Division. These indicators are measures of mortality levels, respectively, in the first year of life (which is most sensitive to development levels) and over the entire lifespan. Data estimates are for 2008.

Maternal mortality ratio. Source: WHO, UNICEF, UNFPA and World Bank. 2005. *Maternal Mortality in 2005: Estimates Developed by WHO, UNICEF, and UNFPA*. Geneva: WHO. This indicator presents the number of deaths to women per 100,000 live births which result from conditions related to pregnancy, delivery and related complications. Precision is difficult, though relative magnitudes are informative. Estimates between 100-999 are rounded to the nearest 10; and above 1,000 to the nearest 100. Several of the estimates differ from official government figures. The estimates are based on reported figures wherever possible, using approaches to improve the comparability of information from different sources. See the source for details on the origin of particular national estimates. Estimates and methodologies are reviewed regularly by WHO, UNICEF, UNFPA, academic institutions and other agencies and are revised where necessary, as part of the ongoing process of improving maternal mortality data. Because of changes in methods, prior estimates for 1995 levels may not be strictly comparable with these estimates.

INDICATORS OF EDUCATION

Male and female gross primary enrolment ratios, male and female gross secondary enrolment ratios. Source: Spreadsheet provided by the UNESCO Institute for Statistics,

April 2008. Population data is based on: United Nations Population Division. 2005/06. *World Population Prospects: The 2006 Revision*. New York: United Nations. Gross enrolment ratios indicate the number of students enrolled in a level in the education system per 100 individuals in the appropriate age group. They do not correct for individuals who are older than the level-appropriate age due to late starts, interrupted schooling or grade repetition. Data are for the most recent year estimates available for the 1999-2007 period.

Male and female adult illiteracy. Source: See gross enrolment ratios above for source; data adjusted to illiteracy from literacy. Illiteracy definitions are subject to variation in different countries; three widely accepted definitions are in use. Insofar as possible, data refer to the proportion who cannot, with understanding, both read and write a short simple statement on everyday life. Adult illiteracy (rates for persons above 15 years of age) reflects both recent levels of educational enrolment and past educational attainment. The above education indicators have been updated using estimates from: United Nations Population Division. 2008. *World Population Prospects: The 2006 Revision*. New York: United Nations. Data are for the most recent year estimates available for the 1995-2004 period.

Proportion reaching grade 5 of primary education.
Source: See gross enrolment ratios above for source. Data are most recent within the school years 1999-2007.

INDICATORS OF REPRODUCTIVE HEALTH

Births per 1,000 women aged 15-19. Source: Spreadsheet provided by the United Nations Population Division. This is an indicator of the burden of fertility on young women. Since it is an annual level summed over all women in the age cohort, it does not reflect fully the level of fertility for women during their youth. Since it indicates the annual average number of births per woman per year, one could multiply it by five to approximate the number of births to 1,000 young women during their late teen years. The measure does not indicate the full dimensions of teen pregnancy as only live births are included in the numerator. Stillbirths and spontaneous or induced abortions are not reflected. Estimates are for the 2005-2010 period.

Contraceptive prevalence. Source: Spreadsheet provided by the United Nations Population Division. These data are derived from sample survey reports and estimate the proportion of married women (including women in consensual unions)

currently using, respectively, any method or modern methods of contraception. Modern or clinic and supply methods include male and female sterilization, IUD, the pill, injectables, hormonal implants, condoms and female barrier methods. These numbers are roughly but not completely comparable across countries due to variation in the timing of the surveys and in the details of the questions. All country and regional data refer to women aged 15-49. The most recent survey data available are cited, ranging from 1986-2007.

HIV prevalence rate, M/F, 15-49. Source: UNAIDS provided data from the United Nations Population Division. 2006. These data derive from surveillance system reports and model estimates. Data provided for men and women aged 15-49 are point estimates for each country. The reference year is 2007. Male-female differences reflect physiological and social vulnerability to the illness and are affected by age differences between sexual partners.

DEMOGRAPHIC, SOCIAL AND ECONOMIC INDICATORS

Total population 2008, projected population 2050, average annual population growth rate for 2005-2010. Source: Spreadsheets provided by the United Nations Population Division. These indicators present the size, projected future size and current period annual growth of national populations.

Per cent urban, urban growth rates. Source: United Nations Population Division. 2008. *World Urbanization Prospects: The 2007 Revision.* CD-ROM Edition: Data in Digital Format. New York: United Nations. These indicators reflect the proportion of the national population living in urban areas and the growth rate in urban areas projected.

Agricultural population per hectare of arable and permanent crop land. Source: Data provided by Food and Agriculture Organization, Statistics Division, using population data based on the total populations from: United Nations Population Division. 2008. *World Population Prospects: The 2006 Revision.* New York: United Nations; and activity rates of economically active population from: ILO. 1996. *Economically Active Population, 1950-2010*, 4th Edition. Geneva: ILO. This indicator relates the size of the agricultural population to the land suitable for agricultural production. It is responsive to changes in both the structure of national economies (proportions of the workforce in agriculture) and in technologies for land development. High values can be related to stress on land productivity and to fragmentation of land holdings. However, the measure is also sensitive to differing development levels and land use policies. Data refer to the year 2005.

Total fertility rate (2008). Source: Spreadsheet provided by the United Nations Population Division. The measure indicates the number of children a woman would have during her reproductive years if she bore children at the rate estimated for different age groups in the specified time period. Countries may reach the projected level at different points within the period.

Births with skilled attendants. Source: Spreadsheet provided by WHO with data from: Database on Skilled Attendant at Delivery. Geneva: WHO. Web site: www.who.int//reproductive-health/global_monitoring/data.html. This indicator is based on national reports of the proportion of births attended by "skilled health personnel or skilled attendant: doctors (specialist or non-specialist) and/or persons with midwifery skills who can diagnose and manage obstetrical complications as well as normal deliveries". Data for more developed countries reflect their higher levels of skilled delivery attendance. Because of assumptions of full coverage, data (and coverage) deficits of marginalized populations and the impacts of chance and transport delays may not be fully reflected in official statistics. Data estimates are the most recent available from 1995 through 2006.

Gross national income per capita. Source: Most recent (2006) figures from: The World Bank. *World Development Indicators Online.* Web site: http://devdata.worldbank.org/dataonline/ (by subscription). This indicator (formerly referred to as gross national product [GNP] per capita) measures the total output of goods and services for final use produced by residents and non-residents, regardless of allocation to domestic and foreign claims, in relation to the size of the population. As such, it is an indicator of the economic productivity of a nation. It differs from gross domestic product (GDP) by further adjusting for income received from abroad for labour and capital by residents, for similar payments to non-residents, and by incorporating various technical adjustments including those related to exchange rate changes over time. This measure also takes into account the differing purchasing power of currencies by including purchasing power parity (PPP) adjustments of "real GNP". Some PPP figures are based on regression models; others are extrapolated from the latest International Comparison Programme benchmark estimates. See original source for details.

Central government expenditures on education and health. Source: The World Bank. *World Development Indicators Online.* Web site: http://devdata.worldbank.org/dataonline/ (by subscription). These indicators reflect the priority afforded to education and health sectors by a country through the government expenditures dedicated to them. They are not sensitive to differences in allocations within sectors, e.g., primary education or health services in relation to other levels, which vary considerably. Direct comparability is complicated by the different administrative and budgetary responsibilities allocated to central governments in relation to local governments, and to the varying roles of the private and public sectors. Reported estimates are presented as shares of GDP per capita (for education) or total GDP (for health). Great caution is also advised about cross-country comparisons because of varying costs of inputs in different settings and sectors. Provisional data are for the most recent year estimates available for 2005.

External assistance for population. Source: UNFPA. 2006. *Financial Resource Flows for Population Activities in 2006*. New York: UNFPA. This figure provides the amount of external assistance expended in 2006 for population activities in each country. External funds are disbursed through multilateral and bilateral assistance agencies and by non-governmental organizations. Donor countries are indicated by their contributions being placed in parentheses. Regional totals include both country-level projects and regional activities (not otherwise reported in the table).

Under-5 mortality. Source: Spreadsheet provided by the United Nations Population Division. This indicator relates to the incidence of mortality to infants and young children. It reflects, therefore, the impact of diseases and other causes of death on infants, toddlers and young children. More standard demographic measures are infant mortality and mortality rates for 1 to 4 years of age, which reflect differing causes of and frequency of mortality in these ages. The measure is more sensitive than infant mortality to the burden of childhood diseases, including those preventable by improved nutrition and by immunization programmes. Under-5 mortality is here expressed as deaths to children under the age of 5 per 1,000 live births in a given year. Estimates are for the 2005-2010 period.

Per capita energy consumption. Source: The World Bank. *World Development Indicators Online*. Web site: http://devdata.worldbank.org/dataonline/ (by subscription). This indicator reflects annual consumption of commercial primary energy (coal, lignite, petroleum, natural gas and hydro, nuclear and geothermal electricity) in kilograms of oil equivalent per capita. It reflects the level of industrial development, the structure of the economy and patterns of consumption. Changes over time can reflect changes in the level and balance of various economic activities and changes in the efficiency of energy use (including decreases or increases in wasteful consumption). Data estimates are for 2005.

Access to improved drinking water sources. Source: WHO and UNICEF. 2007. *Meeting the MDG Drinking Water and*

Sanitation Target: The Urban and Rural Challenge of the Decade. Geneva: WHO. This indicator reports the percentage of the population with access to an *improved source* of drinking water providing an *adequate amount of safe water* located within a *convenient distance* from the user's dwelling. The italicized words use country-level definitions. The indicator is related to exposure to health risks, including those resulting from improper sanitation. Data are estimates for the year 2004.

Editorial Team

The State of World Population 2008

Lead Author/Researcher: Joy Moncrieffe
Editor: Alex Marshall
Culture, Gender and Human Rights Adviser: Azza Karam
Coordinator: Christian Fuersich
Editorial Associate: Triana D'Orazio
Editorial and Administrative Associate: Mirey Chaljub

Acknowledgements:

The Editorial Team expresses its special appreciation to the following
contributors who provided background papers: Alan Greig, Vasantha Kandiah,
Cecilia Maria Bacellar Sardenberg and Maya Unnithan.

A sincere thank you also to the scholars and professionals who provided
valuable comments: Professor Abdullah An-Na'im, Dr. Josef Boehle,
Rabbi Amy Eilberg, Katérina Stenou, Reverend Hans Ucko and Reverend Sister
Francisca Ngozi Uti. Many thanks also go to fellow UNFPA colleagues,
especially Purnima Mane, Mari Simonen and Aminata Toure, Stan Bernstein,
Jose Miguel Guzman, Werner Haug, Kristin Hetle, Abubakar Dungus, Laura
Laski, Nuriye Ortayli, Sherin Saadallah, Saskia Schellekens.

For support to its programmes on culture since 2002, UNFPA wishes to
thank the Swiss government in particular, as well as the German and the
Swedish governments.

United Nations Population Fund
220 East 42nd Street
New York, NY 10017
www.unfpa.org